5o Simple Business Ideas to Make Money

Also By Bernadette Lundall

Half Breed Love
Inner Wisdom and Life Skills [Beginners]
Dana and Daddy

50 Simple Business Ideas to Make Money

Copyright © 2013
Bernadette Lundall

Preface

Fifty Simple Business Ideas to Make Money contains a diversity of practical entrepreneurial ideas that can help one start and establish a unique business venture. It contains some core themes which widen the potential for success. Perhaps the first core theme is that there is a diversity of potential opportunities to make money and increase wealth. This means that business ventures should ideally not resemble one another in the product range and services that is offered. Diversity among businesses actually ensures greater success, particularly among new ventures. It is important that these are not over-concentrated in a geographical market which cannot wholly support or sustain competition between start-ups with the same product range. Diversity in range and type of products and services gives new business ventures a greater chance of success. A kaleidoscope of products and services is therefore better for success than imitating the business next door and trying to offer similar. Therefore it is important to take the time to explore the diversity of potential opportunities which can be established to start a new business.

The second core theme which underpins *Fifty Simple Business Ideas to Make Money* is that successful businesses are demand-driven ventures which respond to real demands in society. Although society is 'out there', it is also a microcosm that is localized within each specific community in which we live. It is an amalgam of intersecting streets and interlinking blocks, populated by people all connected through families, relatives, friends and networks. These communities have a spectrum of unfulfilled demands which established businesses either ignore or find unprofitable to offer at the prices which the people in those communities can afford. By gradually nurturing these demands or needs for services and products, the budding entrepreneur can grow a clientele and establish a business rooted in his/her community. A community is essential to sustain the types of business ideas discussed in this book but once firmly off the ground business ventures along these lines also give character, substance and sustenance to the communities in which they are embedded. The venture built on the demands and needs of society is a self-replicating entity.

The third core theme which permeates *Fifty Simple Business Ideas to Make Money* is best captured by a multiple layer of attributes that is symbolized by the notion of trust. Trust as a notion or category encompasses the relationship between the person venturing out to start a business to make money and the clients and customers that are built up through the process. A relationship of trust is maintained by personal and collective attributes such as honesty, integrity and responsibility. These attributes generate respect which further enriches the trust between the business person and the customer and client. Trust is a network of strength. It is a bond which is fragile to abuse but which is durable and becomes stronger over time when trust as a notion or category becomes a defined quality to the goodwill of the business. As much as the business person is beseeched to direct these attributes that give rise to trust such as honesty, integrity and responsibility to the customers and clients, he/she ought to maintain the same balance with the self and those family members that are directly involved in making the business a success particularly with respect to reward for unpaid labour that is put into the business.

Finally, the business ideas in, *Fifty Simple Business Ideas to Make Money,* requires commitment, sacrifice and hard work to make a new business a success. While the author maps forecasts about the potential earnings that can be derived from various examples of business ventures, these are not quick-fix get rich schemes. Instead, it requires you to put in the hard work long before the successes can be realized. What you need though in abundance is passion to succeed and passion to give the best service to your customers and clients.

VI

Passion will sustain your commitment to the business venture that you choose; it will also anaesthetize you from the pain and sacrifice that you may initially be required to make as well as the temptation to give up before you have reached the turning point where your business gradually starts to show signs of success. Passion will take you through the dark moments when you wish to capitulate but it will also elevate your commitment and determination and confirm that you are on the right track when the achievements of accomplishment gradually flow through.

These four interconnected themes which permeate *Fifty Simple Business Ideas to Make Money* coupled with the highly suggestive practical initiatives it gives, will give the individuals who are planning to start their own business ventures a resource from which to make this start.

Paul Lundall

October 2013

Dear Reader ...

I have written this book for those of you who want to earn an extra income in the informal sector and especially for those of you whose experience has been one of minimal opportunities, basic education and limited skills and money. My aim is to help you turn those disadvantages and challenges into advantages and hard cash.

50 Simple Business Ideas To Make Money contains very basic but fundamentally important ideas. Remember that less is more. The simpler your business idea, the easier it is to execute and the less it costs in cash outlay. The easy business ideas in this book need very little formal skills. So those who have very little skills can still start their own businesses without feeling overwhelmed by business concepts and jargon. This book also caters for potential businessmen/women who have very little capital to invest in a venture. *50 Simple Business Ideas To Make Money* invites you to join the small business community because there is room for you to make money and enjoy a decent standard of living.

Where do you start? Firstly ask, "What is my vision?" Do you want to be debt free in two year's time? Do you want to buy a new car? Do you want to be financially independent? Do you want to have the freedom to travel regularly? Do you want to complete your studies? Do you want to create opportunities for yourself and others? Every person should have a vision for their life. A vision is merely a picture or dream of what you want your life to look like. In order to achieve that vision, picture or dream you need to have a mission. Your mission is **how** you are going to achieve that picture. In other words, which tasks or actions are you going to implement along the way to get closer to your picture, dream or vision.

Once you have set your intention to start your business, always remember that the world is governed by universal laws. The law of

Cause and Effect states that whatever you do, good or bad, is noted and will culminate into a repercussion or consequence. So I urge you from the beginning to ensure that you grow your business foundation from a strong point of honesty and integrity. Remember to be positive and to surround yourself with positive people so that your energy and frequency is always heightened – this will ensure that you draw positivity and success to your business.

Your intuition also plays a vital role in your success as a person and as a businessman/woman. Your intuition is your guide in this lifetime so listen to your instincts, gut or intuition. If it does not feel right then it is not right for you. Never override what you feel. If you do, you will pay dearly for not listening.

Follow your passion and do not chase after the money. The money will come from your passion. Remember that we all have gifts and talents, so use them. Now someone may say that they love singing – singing is their passion but they cannot sing a single note. Remember that the very thing that you are not able to do is the thing that is going to sell. Consult with a voice coach about the different styles of singing and learn the various music terminologies e.g. octaves, C-minor etc. and sing using your untrained strained voice. Avoid going for voice training. Obviously people will laugh and this is exactly the reaction that you desire. People love to laugh because it makes them feel good. So put on a show and charge people to come and enjoy your "singing" abilities. When you do something different people sit up and pay attention. You could make quite a stack of cash! Remember that you do not have to be perfect; you just need passion, honesty and integrity!

I would also like to encourage you dear reader to be kind to yourself and others. Gone are the days of the ruthless businessman/woman. In order to be successful today you need to have boundaries for yourself and others and you need to be considerate of people, animals and the environment. Starting a business requires a lot of positive energy, support and exposure. So if you decide on any of the ideas in this book, remember to do a needs analysis of your market and community, where you take into consideration the needs of the people, animals and environment and build your business according to those needs. Remember that there is **"Power in Asking"** so ask for support, help and favours. Nine times out of ten, people will be very willing to assist where they can. Avoid asking people for money. There are all kinds of bondage in money, which leads to discontent, disrespect and loss of integrity. You do not need that kind of negative energy around you. Remember that you are free to add your own flavour or touch to these business ideas. So go wild and use your creativity to come up with something that will suit your personality, skills and abilities. Enjoy! It's going to be fascinating.

Tips to start your Informal Business

1. Growing wealth and not money

Many people believe that the moment you have some money you need to spend it. Having buying power does not mean that you are wealthy. This is an illusion. I challenge you to observe very wealthy people; they live modest lifestyles. However, they invest their money in projects that create more and more money. *50 Simple Business Ideas To Make Money* is an invitation for you to start creating wealth from a small amount of money. Even if you have a full time job, do something on the side to create some extra cash – this is how you start increasing your bank balance. With this extra cash you will be able to invest in a slightly bigger project/business and become financially liquid. So turn your hobby into a cash generating business or start doing some additional work over weekends to earn extra cash. Remember that *50 Simple Business Ideas To Make Money* was written by a South African, so I would like to encourage you to investigate your own country's currency, market, costing and consumer needs and apply these features to make your business a success.

2. Reading the Market

50 Simple Business Ideas To Make Money demonstrates that you do not need to have special skills or loads of money to start a small business. Look at the needs in your street and community. Sometimes people are not even aware of what their needs are until they are pointed out. For example, the *dog walking business idea;* how many people would have thought that their animals need exercise on a daily or weekly basis? You can educate dog owners about the need and value of walking their pets. When you are able to read the needs in your community you will not only be able to make money but more importantly you will be able to start a movement to educate and conscientise people.

3. The Customer

Never underestimate the intelligence of the customer. This is a common mistake that many businesses make, especially when they start making money. Value the opinion of the customer. Stay in touch with your customer. Your customer is the first person who will inform you of the changing needs of the market. Get customer feedback on a continual basis. Take your customers suggestions seriously because that particular customer will feel valued and will come back for repeat business. This particular customer will also relate their experience to their friends, colleagues and family, which will generate more business for you. Remember that the customer knows the value of their hard earned currency so do not try and milk them for all that they are worth – they will soon cotton on to what you are doing and will choose not to support your business.

4. Costing

Costing is a very important part of any business. Write down the exact value of your material/substance/product. If you do not know the value then you will have to estimate or assess the value of the item/product. Remember to add your labour, electricity and time to the item/product. Once you have a total cost you have to add your profit to the item. This will then give you a total figure, which you will charge your customer. For example, if you are going to bake bread and sell it, you will have to cost the flour, yeast, sugar, salt and water. Work out how many units of electricity you will use to bake a loaf. But remember you can save electricity if you bake four or five loaves at one time. So if you bake five loaves of bread from 2,5kg flour (depending on the type of bread) it will cost you R18 for flour to make five loaves. Yeast will cost R1.80 per packet. To make five loaves you will need 10 packets at a cost of R18.00. For five loaves you will need about half a cup of sugar and about 25ml of salt. Let us estimate that to be about R2.50. Water will cost about 50c. You would probably use about four units of electricity @ R1.20 per unit, which will cost around R4.80. So your total costs to bake five loaves of bread will be R43.80. Remember now you still need to add your profit. So as you can see costing can be quite tricky but vital in order for you to see what it really costs to produce an item and how much money you are actually making in profit.

5. Conservative Forecast

I have deliberately chosen to predict very conservative estimates because the market in each community varies. The effort and the time that each individual puts into their business will vary and so this combination will affect the amount of money generated for each business. *I do not want to give potential business people the impression that you can get rich overnight. The aim of this book is to enable people to get out of their financial difficulties and see that there is in fact light at the end of the financial tunnel.* Remember that your business will be as successful as the amount of time, effort and market identification you put into its foundation.

6. Marketing Tips

1. Word of mouth
2. Referrals
3. Advertising in local and community newspapers
4. Interviews in free magazines
5. Website exposure
6. Blogs
7. Surveys
8. Invite potential customers to a focus group to test your product. Gather honest feedback.

9. Repeat business. Stay in touch with and service your existing customers.
10. Ask a radio station to interview you.
11. Pamphlets and business cards (ask Post Office to distribute)
12. Social media networks (Twitter, Facebook, email etc)
13. Cold calling
14. Place an advertisement on free advertising online sites, e.g. Gumtree, Facebook, Google etc.

If you make an effort to do all fourteen you will be noticed and customers will start making enquiries about your services.

1. A Dog Walking Business

Description

Walking the dogs in your neighbourhood is a very valuable service to pet owners as well as to their dogs who love being exercised.

Outlay

1. Three harnesses (small, medium and large)
2. Three Leashes (small, medium and large)
3. A Bicycle or roller blades (optional)

How, What, Where, When, Who

1. Educate yourself by reading and researching dog owner and dog behaviour. Treat a dog with love and discipline. Let your dog know that you are the Alpha male/female and hence the leader of the pack. Dogs must never walk in front of the dog walker. A dog must walk next to the dog walker.
2. Most dog owners do not have the time to walk their pets. Go from door to door and ask if you can walk their dog. Decide on a price for big dogs, medium sized dogs and small dogs. A fair price is about R20 – R25 per dog per walk. A walk should last not less than 45 minutes. Ask the dog owner how many times a week they would like their dog walked.
3. You would need a bicycle or roller blades if you are walking a very active dog. This dog should run in order to benefit from the exercise. Tie the leash to the bicycle handlebars and cycle. A harness gives you more control. Remember that the shorter the leash, the more control you have over the dog. For safety reasons use a long leash if you are going to use your bicycle or roller blades.

4. Administration – Carry a small hardcover book in which you write each owner's address and the number of times you must walk their dog per week. When you return from your walk the owner should sign that you have walked their dog. Payment should be effected immediately. Indicate which dog and their address you should walk on each particular day so as not to forget which day each dog should be walked.
5. Carry a plastic packet or paper bag in which to pick up all dog droppings on your walk. You do not want to contaminate the neighbourhood because the neighbours will complain and you will lose business that way.
6. Extra services – include in your business picking up dog droppings / pooh in each owners yard. Charge for this service. You could also include washing dogs. Do not cut dogs' hair: that should be left to the professionals. However, you could offer to take the owners dog to the dog groomers/parlour. Also offer to take dogs to the vet. Charge for this extra service.
7. Remember that this is a business so conduct yourself in a professional manner. Remember that every successful business is based on honesty so do not rob the dog or owner of the amount of dog walking time that you have agreed on. Do not do favours for people; you will just create headaches for yourself.

X-Factor: <u>What makes your business different?</u>

1. You are bringing an overseas concept to South Africa and other countries.
2. You offer your dog walking services to people living in complexes and flats.
3. You offer a valuable service to dog owners who are working and do not have the time to walk their pets.

4. You educate your clients about the value of exercising their pets. Your clients will soon notice a positive change in their animals' behaviour.
5. You can walk more than one dog at a time to save time and earn more money.

Forecast

If you walk two dogs per hour and work only half a day, that amounts to eight dogs for four hours work. At R25 per dog that amounts to R200 per day, which amounts to R1000 per week, which amounts to R4000 per month. Not bad at all. You can of cause increase this number by working eight hours per day and remember to include the money you earn from cleaning owners yards, washing their dogs, taking their dogs to the dog groomers and to the vet. This business does not need a large capital outlay and very little is required to invest in the business to keep it going if anything at all. Remember to pay yourself a salary and save the remainder on a monthly basis in order to grow your business in the future.

2. The Computer Man/Woman

Description

The computer man or woman offers a clerical and office service. Many people do not own computers and are not au fait with certain computer programmes.

Outlay

1. A computer
2. A printer (get a copier, fax, scanner – all-in-one printer)
3. Ream of paper
4. Two ink cartridges (black and colour)

How, What, Where, When, Who

1. As the computer man or woman you need to be familiar with a variety of programmes and applications.
2. You will create templates, tables, CV's, convert documents, retrieve documents, post information on the Internet, download information from the Internet, set up email/Twitter/Facebook accounts etc.
3. Advertise your services at conference centres, churches, local and community newspapers, friends, family, work colleagues, the Internet, schools and colleges etc.
4. Give your customers your business card on completion of a job and ask them to refer their friends to you.

X-Factor: What makes your business different?

1. You are able to work fast because you already have templates set up.

2. There is no job too big or too small for you. If you cannot do it, outsource it to someone else and take a percentage of the profit.
3. Teach yourself to design websites and add this service to your portfolio.
4. Host small classes and teach people to become computer literate.
5. Help clients to do their income tax online. You will make a lot of money during the last tax month of the year.
6. Add fax, scanning and copy facilities and Internet access facilities.

Forecast

If you make R50 per day from copying, scanning and faxing – assuming you work six days a week, you will make R1200 per month. If you make R100 per day on other computer services, you will make R2400 per month. If you charge clients R100 to do their income tax online and you service 10 clients per day, you will make R24000 during the income tax month.

3. Art Décor Restorer

Description

Collect, buy and ask for donations of old furniture and household items. Even if it is broken restore it or clean it up and sell it again.

Outlay

1. Sandpaper
2. Varnish and paint
3. Brushes and roller brushes
4. Raw linseed oil
5. Staple gun

How, What, Where, When, Who

1. What to do with old broken furniture? Sand off the old varnish with course sandpaper. Then with smooth sandpaper until you have a smooth finish. Decide if you are going to paint it, re-varnish it, antique it or oil it with raw linseed oil.
2. You might need to change the handles. Perhaps the doors or drawers are in a terrible condition. Educate yourself by reading and researching decoupage art. The wonders of decoupage. Put a coat of wood primer on the area that you want to change. Allow to dry. Paint the desired colour. Glue a picture or pictures that you want on the top or on the doors. Once dry paint entire surface with podge glue. Allow first layer to dry then paint with podge glue again. You can have as many layers of podge glue as you like. The last layer should be Pratley glo glue. Instead of pictures you can use colourfully designed serviettes, glitter or wrapping paper.

3. To change the front of doors you could use a staple gun and staple hessian, fabric or leather to give the door a whole new look.
4. You could also restore old furniture by gluing mirrors or new handles to them. Restore old picture frames by cleaning them with brass or silver cleaner. Use mosaics and tiles to change the surface area of just about any object.
5. Fix old lampshades with interesting fabrics. Reupholster chairs with new fabric using a staple gun.
6. Paint old glassware with glass paint.
7. Antiquing is the art of painting a piece of furniture so that it has an aged effect.
8. Gilt furniture making is the art of painting furniture in metallic paint so that it has the King Louis XVI look.
9. If you are buying second hand or broken furniture remember to bargain.
10. Advertise your services in local newspapers and free magazines. Ask your clients to refer you to their networks.

X-Factor: What makes your business different?

1. Instead of wasting a piece of furniture you are restoring it and lessening wastage on the environment.
2. Your artistic flair will make your pieces unusual and unique.
3. You offer the services of restoration. So clients will bring their items to you to be restored.

Forecast

A second hand table or chest of drawers in poor condition will cost around R750. If you restore it beautifully you could sell it for approximately R3000. The only challenge is the amount of labour/work spent on a piece. However, there is no price for beauty and the outcome is always very rewarding. You could earn more money for restoration work as well.

4. Refrigeration and Stove Painting

Description

> This business is only about restoring the outer appearance of the fridge and stove. Do not work on the mechanics of a refrigerator or stove if you do not have the necessary knowledge and skills.

Outlay

1. A grinder
2. A compressor
3. Paint and primer

How, What, Where, When, Who

1. Restore old fridges and stoves. Sand/grind off the white enamel paint with an electric grinder. It eventually has a silver effect. If your client likes the silver effect your job is done.
2. Some clients want their fridges or stoves to match the colour scheme of their kitchens. Using an electric grinder, sand/grind off the white enamel paint. Use a compressor to paint the fridge/stove the desired colour that the client has chosen.
3. The challenge for this business is to advertise your services. When you see that your clients are happy ask them to refer you to their friends, colleagues and family. Remember that your workmanship needs to be tops in order for people to be satisfied. A satisfied client will always come back and refer you.
4. Remember that the cost of a grinder and compressor will only be a once off cost.

5. Advertise your services at hardware stores, appliance stores and home décor outlets, second-hand furniture stores and kitchen carpentry companies.
6. Ask home décor magazines to showcase your work. This will bring in more business

X-Factor: <u>What makes your business different?</u>

1. Very few people know that they can paint their fridges/stoves various colours.
2. You can go to people's homes to do the work on site. This will save you electricity and transport expenses.

<u>Forecast</u>

If you only refurbish two fridges/stoves a week (conservative estimate) and you charge R1000 per fridge that amounts to R2000 per week, which amounts to R8000 per month. However, if you refurbish one fridge/stove per day, that amounts to R5000 per week, which translates to R20 000 per month. However, in order to achieve this, you really need to market and advertise your business. Always remember to pay yourself a salary, which you should deduct as part of your monthly costs.

5. Collection and Delivery

Description

    Collecting and delivering large items that cannot fit into a car.

Outlay

1. A bakkie/pick-up truck/vanette
2. Rope
3. Salary for a helper
4. Petrol or diesel

How, What, Where, When, Who

1. For a collection and delivery business you would need a bakkie/pick-up truck/vanette and some rope.
2. Go to auctions. After an auction people always look for someone to transport their larger items which cannot fit into their motor vehicles.
3. Offer your services to small businesses such as the refrigeration business. Collection and delivery can sometimes be a headache when the small business and the client do not have the necessary vehicle to transport their larger items. So your client will be the homeowner, the small business person and whoever wants to transport larger items.
4. Remember this is not a courier business.
5. Remember that if you have a bakkie/pick-up truck/vanette you can collect and deliver all kinds of products from household furniture, to garden rubble, to building material to manufactured goods.
6. Decide if it is better to charge a flat rate or a rate based on distance (per kilometre)

X-Factor: <u>What makes your business different?</u>

1. Finding a reliable delivery vehicle can be distressing. You pride yourself on being safe, efficient and reliable.
2. No item is too big or too far to be collected and delivered.
3. You advertise frequently to all second hand furniture stores, auctioneers, appliance repair companies etc.
4. You are visible by the branding and signage on your vehicle.

<u>Forecast</u>

If you make two deliveries per day at R200 per delivery, that amounts to R400 per day, which translates to R2000 per week, which translates to R8000 per month. Remember to deduct your petrol/diesel costs, maintenance on your vehicle and a salary for your helper. Remember to also pay yourself a salary.

6. The Travelling Hairdresser/Stylist

<u>Description</u>

You are a mobile hairdresser. You go to the client's doorstep where you service the client at home or in the workplace.

<u>Outlay</u>

1. Blow dryer
2. Brushes and combs
3. A good shampoo and conditioner
4. A hairdressers scissors (if you are a qualified hairdresser)

<u>How, What, Where, When, Who</u>

1. Focus on one area or suburb. Get one client in each road. Ask your client to tell her/his friends or neighbours about your services. Focusing on one area minimises your travelling costs and time.
2. By going to clients' homes or workplaces you minimize your costs. You save on water and electricity. Do not underestimate the value of doing hair in the workplace. Often a business person needs to go and see a client or has an important meeting but their hair looks greasy or unruly. They may not have had time to go to a salon. You become the emergency hairdresser/hairstylist.
3. If you are a qualified hairdresser/stylist you may offer a range of services. However, if you are not qualified do not offer to cut, colour or treat hair. If you are unqualified but are good at blow drying or braiding these are then the services that you can offer.

4. You do not have to have salon products. Buy a good quality shampoo and conditioner. Often your clients will purchase their own quality hair products.
5. If you are unqualified and want to further yourself in this business, I suggest and encourage you to educate yourself further by attending hairdressing school and reading and researching the latest hair trends.
6. You would need a motor vehicle and money for petrol or if you do not own a vehicle you would need bus fare or taxi fare.

X-Factor: What makes your business different?

1. There are many elderly or sick people at home who need to have their hair done.
2. You could offer your services to retirement homes and frail care centres.
3. You save the parent lots of time by doing all their children's hair on one particular day.
4. The client who uses your services saves at least 25% of what they would spend at a hair salon.

Forecast

If you charge R75 for a blow dry and you service four clients per day that amounts to R300 per day, which translates to R1500 per week, which translates to R6000 per month. Remember that this is a conservative calculation and does not include other services such as braiding, colour treating etc. Remember to deduct your salary and other costs. Save the remainder or reinvest it into your business.

7. Stoep Kombuis (Veranda Kitchen)

Description

This home restaurant is a very simple concept. You invite people to your home to enjoy traditional homemade food.

Outlay

1. Old table and six chairs
2. Food ingredients
3. Crockery and cutlery for six
4. Advertising

How, What, Where, When, Who

1. Get an old table and six chairs. Serve not more than two dishes. Serve a dish that people enjoy across the board. Serve something that will attract foreign visitors as well as those looking for a local experience. Mince curry and Vetkoek (fried bread) or Vetkoek and jam. Perhaps milk tart for dessert. Serve tea and coffee.
2. Vetkoek is not something that you can buy from a restaurant or takeaway outlet. However, it is a traditional South African cuisine enjoyed by all across the board.
3. The idea of a stoep kombuis is to bring people together especially those who do not know one another. This is a wonderful way for strangers to come together and sit at the same table. People get to know one another this way and become friends.
4. Go to the tourism board and enquire if you can register your services there. Leave pamphlets at airports, train stations and with mini bus and meter taxis as well as libraries and churches.

5. Ensure that you know the history of your community or town as tourists might want to know more about the local area. Tell stories about your family, neighbourhood and community. People love hearing stories.
6. Make sure that your garden or yard is tidy and has enough greenery. Make sure that you have a launch or invite important people in your community in order to give your business a jumpstart.
7. Remember to keep it simple.

X-Factor: What makes your business different?

1. Bringing strangers together to sit at one table and become friends.
2. Marketing traditional South African (or your own country) food to locals and foreigners.
3. Providing a home away from home concept so that whomever uses your services feels as welcome as they would in their own home.

Forecast

If you serve six people per day and each person spends R25 and your business is open seven days a week you will make R4200 per month. Not bad at all, especially if you do not have a job. Remember that you could service more than six people per day. The above is merely a very conservative estimate.

8. Informal Auctioneer

Description

An informal Auctioneer auctions goods to the highest bidder.

Outlay

1. An auctioneer's hammer or a bell
2. A large room or garage in which to store your goods and from which to host your auction

How, What, Where, When, Who

1. Educate yourself about the rules, duties and responsibilities of an auctioneer. You can find this information on the internet and through literature.
2. Use your back yard or garage. Invite your community members who are in need of cash to bring their items to your auction. This must be done at least two days prior to the auction so that the items can be registered and logged. This simply means that you need to write down the item for sale and the estimated price that the owner wants.
3. You can also appraise the item. This means that you use your common sense and knowledge to give the item a value. Remember that people who attend auctions are looking for a bargain. Bargain hunting can be a very thrilling and satisfying experience. Do not underestimate the drive that a bargain hunter has – in other words the excitement makes them push up the price.
4. The auctioneer normally takes a percentage of the sale price. Investigate what that percentage is by phoning established auctioneers and asking them.

5. Remember that people who attend an auction need to pay a deposit upon entry. This ensures that when they conclude a bid they have money to pay. If they have not bought anything return their deposit money. These transactions should be documented and recorded and attendees should be given a receipt.
6. The auctioneer could have one or two auctions a week but they should always be on the same days so that people become familiar with the days and times.
7. Attend a formal auction so that you become familiar with procedures first before you start your business.
8. This business has no capital outlay if it is done informally. However, you will need to pay for costs such as space (even if it's your garage space), electricity etc. You may need one or two helpers who should be paid.

X-Factor: What makes your business different?

1. You are guaranteed to enjoy the thrill and the rush of making a sale.
2. There is no capital outlay.
3. You will gain valuable business and appraisal skills.
4. This informal business could turn into a more formal business or you may have gained enough knowledge and skills to work for an established auctioneer.

Forecast

It is very difficult to predict the forecast for this business as you do not know what the items are that are to be auctioned. But for estimation sake let's assume that each item you auction is auctioned for R100 and you have ten items to auction. If your commission is 10% then you will earn R10 for each item. So you will make R100 for each auction. If you host two auctions a week you will earn R200 per week, which translates into R800 per month. Remember that this is a very conservative estimate.

9. Network Marketing

Description

> Sell health or cosmetic products. Find a reputable company with proven scientific evidence of their product. Find a company that will pay you commission **and** bonuses. You must receive free ongoing training from this company. If you only get once off training that is not good enough as you will need constant support and fresh ideas to sell your products. Network marketing is a great business to manage part-time.

Outlay

1. A positive attitude
2. A telephone
3. Communications skills – the ability to speak to people
4. A network of people – church congregations, work colleagues, neighbours, friends and family, social networks (Internet), friends of friends, employers
5. Your initial start-up pack of sample products

How, What, Where, When, Who

1. Host parties or information sessions at home, at a friend's house, at church, at work, in hospital/clinic waiting rooms where you explain the benefits of approximately six products.
2. Allow potential customers to sample products. Do not bore people with too much information.
3. Ask people what health issues they want assistance with and talk about those products that speak to their particular health issue.
4. Find people who have health issues and speak to them on an individual basis about the benefits of your products.

5.   Remember there is money to be made in repeat business. Service your regular customers.

X-Factor: What makes your business different?

1. Every business requires an X-factor to differentiate it from other similar businesses. If you are going to sell health products, concentrate on the four or five major illnesses such as diabetes, high blood pressure, arthritis, obesity, cancer and skin disorders. Your product may be able to improve these conditions.
2. Test these products on your own or family's illness. You could use this positive experience in your sales pitch.
3. If you decide to sell cosmetics, sell hypoallergenic natural products. Preferably also products made from scientifically researched herbs and plants.
4. Offer your customers a prize or sample if they purchase over a certain amount.
5. If you sell weight loss products, get your customers to compete with one another and offer a prize for the one who loses the most weight in the shortest time etc.
6. People love being acknowledged so make your customers feel special by giving them a thank you note, birthday card or gift with your business card and list of latest products.

Forecast

A profit in this business depends entirely on the number of people you convince to buy your product. However, if you have a good proven product, the product will speak for itself and you would not have to do much convincing. If you only work weekends and sell to six people who each buy two products, you could easily earn R1000 per weekend. That's R4000 per month. Not bad...If however, you decide to work full time you could easily earn R15000 – R20000 per month.

10. Meals for Singles

Description

Have you ever made a meal for one person? It is one of the hardest things to do. You put all that activity into one thing and then you have to eat it alone. Many people do not enjoy going to a restaurant to eat all alone. Most people who are recently divorced, separated or single through the loss of a loved one will tell you that their eating habits suffer and become unhealthy. So this business is about providing healthy meals for single people. However, this does not mean that you exclude people who are not single.

Outlay

1. Hygienic kitchen
2. Fresh food ingredients
3. Printed menu's
4. Telephone

How, What, Where, When, Who

1. Work out a menu that consists of healthy food from at least three different food groups.
2. Provide three main courses to choose from. So if a customer comes three times per week to buy your product he/she will not be eating the same thing.
3. Provide two desserts to choose from.
4. Change your menu every week. So you will have four menus for the month.
5. Provide cool foods in summer and warm foods in winter.
6. Ensure that your ingredients are seasonal and that they are fresh.

7. Provide safe recyclable packaging. Explore the dangers of using certain plastics in which to store food.
8. Advertise your services in local newspapers, the Internet and by word of mouth. Leave pamphlets and business cards with local divorce attorneys in your area, funeral parlours as well as supermarkets, butcheries and car parks.
9. Speak to people and tell them about your concept.
10. Get to know your regular customers and tell them about your specials. Also ask your customers which meals they would prefer for special occasions.
11. Provide vegetarian options and healthy food for diabetics.
12. Take orders in advance so that you do not have food left over.
13. Educate yourself on healthy food choices, calories and portion sizes so that you can help your customers make better food choices.

X-Factor: <u>What makes your business different?</u>

1. Remember to keep it simple.
2. Deliver your pre-packaged food to your regulars or to their work places.
3. Allow customers to bring their own dishes or containers – this will save you the packaging costs.
4. 'Kill two birds with one stone'. Provide vegetarian and diabetic safe food that everyone can eat. This saves you having to make alternative or extra dishes. By doing this you will still have healthy food that everyone can enjoy.
5. Include a telephone service. Allow customers to place their orders via telephone before 12 noon and collect their orders on their way from work.

Forecast

If you charge R25 for a meal and R12 for dessert (you need to do a proper costing) and you have five customers per day and you only work week days, you will make R3700 per month. If you deliver your product remember to charge a delivery fee. This is obviously a very conservative estimate and with more advertising you can draw more clients.

11. A Brewing Business

Brewing your own drinks can be such a fun and exciting business. The start-up costs of this business are unbelievably low. This is a business that can grow into a Multi-million Rand Corporation. But remember to start off small, keep it simple and grow your business steadily. The most cost effective drink to start off with is ginger beer.

<u>Outlay</u>

1. Dish towel
2. A bucket and long wooden spoon
3. Water
4. Ginger powder or fresh ginger
5. Sugar
6. Yeast
7. Bottles for bottling

<u>How, What, Where, When, Who</u>

1. All your ingredients are placed in the bucket which is covered with the clean dish towel. The brewing and fermentation process is now under way. Do not seal the bucket as it might explode from the gases.
2. You can get an assortment of ginger beer recipes off the internet. Attempt a few and decide which one suits you and your customers' best. You could invite some friends and family over for a tasting party.
3. This tasting party is also a marketing exercise.
4. Once you have decided on the winning recipe, make your ginger beer, do your costing of the ingredients and equipment.

5. Remember that for your next batch you will not need to include all your equipment in your costing procedure again. You will only need to cost your ingredients and your bottles.
6. Find out what commercial ginger beer costs at your local store and charge slightly less. Remember to include your profit.
7. Start a sales drive in your street, then your community bazaars, fairs, holistic markets, churches, schools, parties and shopping centres. Remember that there are many tired, thirsty people at taxi ranks and railway stations.

Growing this business further

1. If you develop a flair and passion for this business then you need to educate yourself further. Do a few courses in the craft of brewing.
2. Join a brewer's community in person and on the Internet.
3. Invest in a professional brewer's kit, which ranges from R1000 upwards.
4. Experiment with different brews such as fruit wines, liquors, mampoer and witblits (Schnapps)
5. Experiment with spices and wood.
6. Investigate the liquor laws of the country so that you do not get into any trouble.
7. Remember that if you sell your product commercially you will be subject to health inspection of your premises and equipment.
8. The possibilities of this business are endless and the learning never stops.
9. Create ready to pour cocktails in a bottle or can.

X-Factor: <u>What makes your business different?</u>

1. Try Jamie Oliver's instant ginger beer recipe.
2. Find a replacement solution for sugar.
3. Make healthy ginger beer from xylitol instead of sugar so that you include and consider the health of diabetics and health conscious people. This is a huge chunk of the market that remains untapped.
4. Consider healthy non-alcoholic fruit brews.
5. Design a special or different bottle. The current market accommodates 1,5 and 2 litre bottles. Can you think of something different?
6. Create your own label. Remember it must be something that resonates with your market and is recognizable by your customers.
7. Host your own classes where you teach others to make home brews.

<u>Forecast</u>

If you charge R10 for a bottle of ginger beer and you sell six bottles per day and you sell seven days a week; you will make R1680 per month. However do not forget the sales you make from markets, fares, family and friends. You could increase your profit by selling cups of ginger beer instead of bottles to passers by. Not to mention the added income from your brewing classes and the status of becoming a brew master.

12. Chocolatier

Just about everybody loves chocolate. So you need not convince people about your product. The question is how are you going to make your chocolate different and which untapped market are you going to tap into?

Outlay

1. Chocolate
2. Moulds
3. Refrigerator
4. Added ingredients

How, What, Where, When, Who

1. For the most part people are accustomed to sweet chocolate.
2. The dark bitter chocolate market is largely untapped in this country. Most people would use dark chocolate to bake.
3. Educate yourself on the origin of chocolate and where and how cocoa beans are grown. Acquiring some historical knowledge can be very beneficial.
4. Find two excellent chocolate recipes on the internet. One for sweet and the other for dark chocolate.
5. Attend a chocolate making workshop and visit a reputable chocolate factory to see how their products are made.
6. Begin by making small batches of chocolate.
7. Have a tasting survey amongst various groups of people such as university students, old age homes, schools, crèches and hospitals.
8. Ask detailed questions in your survey. Is the chocolate smooth, sweet enough, too sweet? Do you like plain chocolate or would you prefer fruit, nuts, chilli or biscuit

wafers? Is there anything else that you would like in your chocolate? How about savoury chocolate?

9. Document your feedback and use this information to improve your product.

X-Factor: <u>What makes your business different?</u>

1. Teach people the art of making chocolate. Host chocolate-making parties for kids and adults.
2. Become creative and invent something different that becomes uniquely South African, e.g. biltong dipped in chocolate; bread dipped in chocolate or chocolate pap/porridge sauce.
3. Supply your customers with chocolate gift packs, cards with a chocolate inside, chocolate lunch packs or chocolate bars.
4. Improve and market dark chocolates; this is a largely untapped market in South Africa. Just about everybody in Europe prefers dark 'bitter' chocolate.
5. Consider lactose intolerant people and vegans and use another product instead of milk in your chocolate.
6. Sell specific chocolates for religious, public and celebratory holidays, e.g. Easter and St Valentine's Day.

<u>Forecast</u>

If you sell 10 bars of chocolate per day at R10 a bar, you could make R100. If you work six days a week you could earn R600, which translates into R2400 per month. There is more profit to be made in teaching chocolate-making and being innovative about your business.

13. Candle Making and Accessories

Candle making is such an easy versatile craft. You could go to a candle making workshop, get a book from the library or learn this craft off the Internet.

<u>Outlay</u>

1. Wax
2. Wicks and wick pins
3. Moulds
4. Melting Pot
5. Thermometer
6. Pour pot
7. Scale to weigh your wax
8. Hammer to break wax
9. Candle wax dye

<u>How, What, Where, When, Who</u>

1. Firstly, learn to make a plain white candle.
2. Ensure that you use quality wax and wicks.
3. Learn to make different colour candles with candle wax dye, scented candles with pure aromatic oils, beeswax and soy candles, container and votive candles.
4. Be very careful when melting hot wax and do make sure that children are not close by.
5. Make candles of all sizes.
6. Display your candles with all the same colours grouped together.
7. Sell your candles to churches, temples, event companies, house and home stores etc.

8. Ask the manager of a busy shopping mall if you could display your product on a table near a food outlet. People usually queue at a food outlet and they are bound to notice your stall.

X-factor: <u>What makes your business different?</u>

1. Include a pamphlet on safety precautions when burning candles.
2. Invent a candle holder base that can be filled with water so that if the burning candle topples over it is extinguished by the water.
3. Sell candle holders made from recycled material.
4. Make a candle holder that can hold seven candles in a circle, which can be used as a centre piece on a dining table. That way you sell seven candles to one customer.
5. Sell candle lighters and candle extinguishers. There is nothing worse than burning your fingers when a lighted match burns to the last bit. And probably a little worse than that is blowing out a candle and inhaling the smoke fumes.
6. Sell packs of the same colour candles and packs with various colour candles but with different sizes. That way you are selling at least six candles to one customer.
7. Sell your candles to an overseas market and let your customers know that a percentage of your profits go to the feeding and support of a hungry child in Africa. Honour this agreement and sponsor a disadvantaged child in your community.

<u>Forecast</u>

Suppose you work six days a week and sell ten individual candles per day at R20 per candle. If you sell two candle packs per day at R100 each and if you sell two candle holders per day at R25 each you will make a sum of R2700 per week, which translates to R10800 per month. Not bad for a small business.

14. Curtains and Bedding

The only skill you need here is to be able to sew in a straight line. You can learn this skill. Other than that you will need to utilize your common sense, creativity and a little arithmetic. Most curtain lengths come in standard sizes so ensure that you know the standard sizes. Remember that in order to create an illusion of opulence and extravagance, use more fabric for extra gathers and a longer length (this applies to curtains and duvet covers).

Outlay

1. Sewing machine
2. Over locker machine

How, What, Where, When, Who

1. Learn to know the different types of fabrics, e.g. taffeta, organza, linen, netting, Dutch lace, velvet etc and how these fabrics fall to the floor.
2. Two types of sheets, a fitted sheet and a flat sheet.
3. Duvet covers.
4. Visit various fabric stores and ask questions and advice about the latest fashion fabrics.
5. Visit hotels and guest houses and look at their curtaining and bedding. Ask their managers/owners who their suppliers are. Ask if they would like any extra attention to detail regarding their curtaining and bedding.
6. Conduct research on historical/period curtaining styles. Incorporate these period styles with modern trends.
7. Stage curtaining with a twist.

8. Advertise your product to private individuals, guest houses, hotels and event companies (personalize your product for their clients, e.g. bridal couple's names).
9. Hospitals, large care facilities and prisons also use curtaining and bedding.

X-Factor: What makes your business different?

1. Create a brand name or logo for your company. Embroider this on your sheets and pillow cases.
2. Embroider personalized bedding and towels for teenagers, children and couples.
3. Create sexy curtains with see through and lacy undertones.
4. Instead of using rope cords to tie curtains together create sexy curtain underwear to tie curtains together.
5. Take orders from clients where they bring their own fabric and cotton.

Forecast

If you work five days a week and sell two sets of curtains at R600 per set, two personalized towels at R50 each and two sets of sheets at R120 per set daily, you will make R1540 per day, which translates to R30800 per month. Now that is not bad at all.

15. Freedom of the Shaven Head

The shaven head is totally in fashion nowadays. Men, women and children are opting for the shaven head. It is much more cost effective to shave your head than to go to a barber or hairdresser. The customer saves money that would have been used for hair care products and treatments. It is so liberating to have a shaven head and not have to worry about ruining your hairdo.

Outlay

1. Covering/Cloak
2. Hair clipper
3. Barber's blade
4. Shaving cream
5. Sterilizing liquid
6. A few towels

How, What, Where, When, Who

1. All you have to do all day long is shave heads and clean your equipment.
2. Make sure that you offer a respectable service to men, women and children as this is becoming a growing trend with women as well.

X-Factor: What makes your business different?

1. Offer a ten minute head massage after you have shaven the customer. Use cream or good quality oil. This is such a relaxing experience that people will come to you simply for this service. Do a bit of research on aromatherapy oils and massage techniques.

2. If you are shaving someone with long hair ask your customers permission to donate their hair to the Cancer Foundation or a cancer organization in order to have wigs made. Your customers will see that you have a social consciousness and will recommend you to future customers.
3. Some people might not want their heads shaven but might just come for the head massage. Charge a different rate for this.

Forecast

If you work six days a week and you shave eight heads per day at a cost of R30 per head, you will earn R5760 per month. Once your reputation starts preceding you, you can shave 15 heads a day and earn R10800 per month but remember the massage service is what will draw people to your business.

16. Dating/Match-Making Service

Gone are the days where men and women were formally introduced through societal balls and formal functions. Internet dating can be such a harrowing if not a downright disappointing experience, so why not start a dating/match making service? Love is something that never goes out of fashion and we are all looking for Mr/Ms Right.

Outlay

1. Interviewing space/room
2. Questionnaire
3. Pen and paper
4. Telephone

How, What, Where, When, Who

1. This is a business that requires honesty, integrity and a deep level of respect for your client and an even deeper measure of confidentiality.
2. You will need a space to interview your client. If you do not have a private space then you will have to interview your client in a coffee shop or restaurant, which will cost money because you will have to order food or drink.
3. Use your observation skills and intuition to the best of your ability. What is your first impression of the client? How do they carry themselves? Are they confident? Do they smile or fidget a lot? Are they easy going or uptight?
4. Now the interview begins. Ask pertinent questions. In fact draw up a questionnaire. Does this client have a life of their own? Are they educated? Do they have a vision for their lives? What successes have they achieved? How have they managed their challenges and setbacks? Are they independent

or needy? What are their interests and general knowledge? What does the client want in a potential partner – they must be very specific?

5. Your client needs to provide you with a current photograph. All this confidential information is kept in a client portfolio.
6. Once you have about ten clients on your list you can start matching your clients with one another.
7. You have to do the advertising to invite clients onto your books.
8. What kind of client market are you looking at? Do you want to match make only professionals? Do you want to match make only a certain age group? Do you want to match make only heterosexual couples?
9. Charge your fee and offer perhaps three dates if the first two were unsuccessful. If the first one or two dates were successful your client will forfeit the third date.
10. Always ensure the safety of your clients; your business reputation depends on that.

X-Factor: What makes your business different?

1. You may decide to match make older men with younger women.
2. You may decide to specialize in cross-cultural match making.
3. You may be open to match making gay clients or clients with other orientations.
4. You may decide to specialize in match making foreign brides for local men.
5. You may decide to offer a makeover service for a client that has potential but whose appearance lacks the "X-factor".
6. You may decide to collaborate with a life coach to help a client get over a past relationship and move forward.
7. You may facilitate a dinner where your clients can mingle and meet in a safe environment.

8. Remember that some clients would prefer to pay for every date that you set up instead of a package deal.
9. You offer a personal touch, which online dating does not.
10. By personally screening your clients, you are able to root out the unsavoury characters.

Forecast

You need to do a proper costing of your service but if for example your fee is R450 to set up three dates and you work five days a week and you see two clients per day, you will earn R18000 per month. Remember to deduct all your costs, especially your advertising costs.

17. Indigenous/Home Remedies Project

This business will suit someone who has an affinity for healing and an interest in indigenous/home remedies. If you are fortunate enough you may have inherited a book with home remedies from a parent or grandparent. If not, collect remedies from family and friends and compile these historic treasures for the next generation.

Outlay

1. Paper and pens
2. Voice recorder
3. Telephone
4. Some knowledge of and interest in home remedies

How, What, Where, When, Who

1. This book will become a proudly South African (or your own country) heritage.
2. Research indigenous Khoi/San/Xhosa/Zulu/Dutch/ and English remedies (or your own indigenous country roots)
3. Divide the book into sections a) Medicinal Remedies b) Household hints and tips c) Spiritual Rites and Rituals e.g. pray for rain, protection, luck and love.
4. Archival research.
5. Oral interviews
6. Travelling to all corners of the country.
7. Sponsorship to conduct research.
8. This work will culminate into a revival of ancient and traditional lore, which for the most part is lost to the present generation.
9. Workshops, classes and conversations about ancient and traditional medicine.

10. Retreats and expeditions into remote areas, forests and deserts to explore plant life and to experience the power of ritual.
11. The generation of book sales/money to be used to sponsor a student in the study of homeopathy, chemistry or some form of complimentary or alternative medicine.

X-Factor: What makes your business different?

1. This book has social responsibility connotations and will suit someone who has historical, academic or activist tendencies and interests.
2. This project will spiral into various sub-projects and may even become an NGO or social organization.
3. Retreats and expeditions to historical sites can become a tourist attraction.
4. Invite school children/youth on these expeditions to reconnect with their roots.

Forecast

This project can become the beginning of so many great things and it begs the attention of someone who is willing, courageous and strong enough to take this vision unashamedly forward. I wish you well with this venture.

18. Trash for Cash

Collecting trash and recycling it so that your end product is sold for cash. This is a largely untapped market in South Africa. Your product is trash, which is readily and freely available. Remember your market does not have to be local and you do not have to concentrate on one product.

Outlay

1. Transport such as a bakkie or small lorry.
2. Telephone
3. An empty space such as a large room, yard or garage

How, What, Where, When, Who

1. Decide what type of trash you are going to collect.
2. Glass, paper, plastic, household junk, metal, aluminium etc.
3. This business can have different facets, e.g. collection and distribution of trash, recycling of trash into reusable by-products, sale of household junk to the public so that they can recycle it.
4. Glass items can be recycled into new glass items, paper can be recycled into packaging, plastic can be recycled into new plastic products, aluminium can be recycled for manufacturing purposes.
5. Household "junk" can be recycled into craft items, e.g. recycle an old dinner plate into a clock, recycle old boots into pot plant holders; old bowls can be recycled into hand basins etc.
6. It is best to do research into recycling so that you can decide on the best part of the recycling process to enter.
7. Remember that there are various markets as well as local and foreign markets that you can tap into.

43

8. Research successful recycling companies in South Africa (or your own country) and abroad in order to get an idea of what you can do.

X-Factor: <u>What makes your business different?</u>

1. You are not going to pull your nose up at any trash. Remember that trash is cash.
2. You will be serving the environment in a positive way.
3. You will create jobs for others.
4. Educate South Africans or your countrymen to keep their environment clean.
5. Teach households to separate their garbage into glass, plastic and paper bags.
6. Collect old used motor and cooking oil. Start a depot where used oil can be dropped. Sell this used oil for bio fuel manufacturing.
7. Investigate what by-products can be made from rubber tyres.
8. Most recycling businesses are invisible to the public so become visible so that the public can relate to what recycling is all about. Reach one, teach one!

<u>Forecast</u>

This business can become so vibrant and can reach so many corners of society; however, it also depends on the vision and foresight of the business owner. It is rather difficult to forecast cash generation for this business so I would encourage you to research three recycling companies and find out what their profit margins were in their first, second and third years. Also research what their major stumbling blocks were so that you can learn from this. Make sure that you adhere to your city's by-laws around trash and the sale of trash.

19. Cute Stationery

Create stationery with an artistic flair. Now you do not have to be artistic you just have to be creative. You can also do craft work on your stationery. This is a multi million dollar industry in America.

Outlay

1. Coloured paper and pens
2. Coloured card paper.
3. Paint
4. Calligraphy pens
5. Computer
6. Camera
7. Photocopy machine
8. Guillotine

How, What, Where, When, Who

1. Design different types of envelopes, perhaps with different colour flaps, with drawn or painted flowers, hearts, stripes, dots, geometric shapes, animals etc.
2. Paint kiddie style, stick men, doodle, sketch etc any adult can do this.
3. Photograph your painting then transfer to your computer and create a zoom image or a watermark image.
4. Think of how a kid communicates and use these sayings as poetry on your stationery.
5. Stationery could include envelopes, writing pads, note pads, book markers, kiddie colouring books and children's stationery.

X-Factor: <u>What makes your business different?</u>

1. The use of art from a child's perspective.
2. Imperfection is sold as though it is the cutest thing ever.
3. Remember to paint or draw the way a child would. That is the very thing that will grab the customers' attention.
4. Go to crèches and schools and ask permission to purchase kiddie artwork and use these priceless pieces in your stationery.
5. Sell individual items but also sell a combo pack.

<u>Forecast</u>

If you work six days a week and sell four combo packs per day at R100 per pack and individual items amounting to R100 per day you will earn R3000 per week, which translates to R12000 per month. That is a decent amount of money for "imperfect" art stationery.

20. Funeral Event Consultant

Death is a part of life and during the period of loss, family members are in shock and traumatised and are not able to think clearly much less make sound decisions. The task of the funeral consultant is to assist the family in making decisions and sourcing the best service providers for the family.

Outlay

1. Transport
2. Telephone
3. Portfolio with pictures of coffins and prices of funerals from various funeral parlours
4. A network of service providers (Organist, caterer, venues, florist, singers/soloist, musicians, photographer/videographer, photocopy and printing shops, inter-denominational ministers, hearses, car rental companies etc.)

How, What, Where, When, Who

1. Ask a number of funeral parlours if you can consult for them and bring the business to the public's doorstep.
2. Your client is not the funeral parlour but the client. Your job is to give the client the best deal that they can afford so working for many funeral parlours gives the client more options.
3. You will not need an office because you will visit the client in their homes. Generally funeral parlours only give their clients one or two options e.g. choosing an outfit for the deceased can add to the cost of a funeral. The funeral consultant can suggest that the deceased be laid to rest in their own clothes, perhaps a favourite garment or suit.

4. Know the laws regarding burial, cremations and embalming. Find out if anyone can officiate at a funeral.
5. Educate yourself on the rites and rituals of funerals for all religions.
6. The cost and arrangements regarding the transportation of a body to and from various parts of the world.

X-Factor: What makes your business different?

1. Your contracts and transactions will be with people from many faiths.
2. You have a network of service providers so the family does not have to scurry around looking for service providers.
3. You can offer a family many options to choose from.
4. You assist your clients with insurance and burial policies as well as insurance claims.
5. You create business opportunities for other micro entrepreneurs in your community.

Forecast

If you arrange four funerals per week and your cut is R1000 per funeral, you will earn R4000 for the week which translates to R16000 per month. However your percentage cut will be determined by the host funeral parlour and this should be negotiated. The family will pay for most of the services provided and those charges do not come from the costs of the funeral itself.

21. The Waterhole

Water is the most underrated drink in the world. The human body can only be deprived of water for seven days. After seven days the body's organs start shutting down. Most people do not drink enough water and in fact suffer from dehydration.

Outlay

1. Water
2. Purifier
3. Bottles (glass or plastic)
4. Cups (styrofoam or plastic)

How, What, Where, When, Who

1. Get a good purification system, preferably something you can attach to a tap.
2. Who needs water? Everybody! Sportsmen/women, women, men, children, plants and animals.
3. Sell bottled water, water in cups and large containers of water.
4. You will find your clients at holiday places, the beach, sports events, schools, camping places, construction sites, restaurants and food outlets etc.

X-Factor: What makes your business different?

1. Educate yourself about the healing properties of water.
2. Teach people about detoxing and healing with water. Create information brochures.
3. Teach people about the scarcity of water and inform them about water saving techniques.

4. Sell water saving shower heads and tap purification devices.
5. Add fresh parsley, mint and lemon in small quantities to water. Never use flavourants and additives; the law considers this to be a cool drink.

<u>Forecast</u>

If you sell water at two events per week and you sell 100 bottles of water at R5 per bottle at each event, you will make R1000 per week, which translates to R4000 per month. Remember that you will also make money from your water workshops and water saving and purification devices.

22. The Juice Bar

Everyone loves juice and we all know about the health aspects of drinking juice infused with spices, herbs, fruit and vegetables. However this can become a time consuming and messy task for the individual.

Outlay

1. A good quality industrial juicer
2. Cups and bottles in assorted sizes
3. Spices, herbs, fruit and vegetables

How, What, Where, When, Who

1. Educate yourself on the healing properties of juicing and the combinations of spices, herbs, fruit and vegetables that aid various ailments and parts of the body.
2. Begin by marketing your product with your friends and family. Ask them to refer you to their family, friends and colleagues.
3. Host tasting functions and charge an entry fee. Ask your customers what they think of your juice combinations. Ask your customers to suggest new juice combinations.
4. Take orders and include a delivery fee.
5. Communicate with your clients and ask if they have any particular health issues. Then recommend which juice combination they should drink.
6. Ask big companies if you can sell to their staff.
7. Get to know your clients and observe their health from the exterior; use this information to recommend which juice combination they should drink.

X-Factor: <u>What makes your business different?</u>

1. Your fresh ingredients make your business unique.
2. Your spice, herb, fruit and vegetable combinations make your business unique.
3. Host juice combination workshops where clients combine their own juices.
4. Introduce juicing as an alternative to cool drinks for children.
5. Host juice combination workshops for children and teens where there are high levels of participation.
6. Introduce your concepts to teens as a cool, radical and fashionable thing to do.
7. Include the ancient healing properties of aloe and apple cider vinegar in your juice.
8. Introduce fruit and vegetable smoothies.
9. Blend certain ingredients for weight-loss and detoxing.
10. Brand your business for its uniqueness.

<u>Forecast</u>

If you sell 20, 250ml cups at R7 per cup and 20, 350ml bottles per day at R10 per bottle daily, you will make R2040 per week if you work six days a week. This translates to R8160 per month. Remember that you will make more money at tasting events, workshops and at large companies. Remember the healing factor (what clients want) of this business as well as the labour intensity (what clients do not want to do) is what will make people support your concept.

23. Private Lessons/Tuition

This business requires you to have excellent skills in your field of expertise. Human beings are not stagnant beings and constantly want to learn and improve themselves. Private lessons can be offered to children, adults and the workforce. Decide what your field of expertise is and use your passion for this field to teach others.

Outlay: [Depending on your type of business]

1. Computer
2. Textbooks
3. White board
4. Large room
5. Table and chairs
6. Dance shoes

How, What, Where, When, Who

1. If you have an affinity for mathematics offer private lessons in mathematics. Approach the parents in your neighbourhood and ask them to sign up their kids if they have difficulty with mathematics. Go to your nearest schools and ask the principal if you can advertise your services to the school population.
2. If you have an affinity for computers offer private computer lessons. We are living in such an advanced information age that those who are not computer literate will be the ones who do not get the jobs that they desire. You can include an added service of writing and designing your clients' CVs.
3. Dance and exercise classes. Many people have a bucket list and learning to dance may be one of the items on their list. Many people want private/individual exercise sessions but feel too intimidated to join a gym. You can offer to go to their

homes to teach them how to exercise their various muscle groups by just using their bodies and the furniture in their homes.

4. Approach large companies and offer to teach their staff to dance during their lunch hour. Dancing is a huge stress buster and helps people to become more focused, disciplined and productive in the long term.

X-Factor: <u>What makes your business different?</u>

1. The personal touch and the individual attention make your business unique. However, this does not mean that you should host a class with one client. You can conduct a class with more than one person but remember to give each client individual attention.
2. Your passion for your subject/field must make your classes come 'alive'! Your clients must feel that they can not wait for the next class.
3. Your lessons must be very interactive and client participation is of the utmost importance. Watch out for the client who wants to be the 'teachers pet'. Remember people are paying you for a service and for your individual attention.
4. When your students succeed as a result of your tuition they will certainly tell others about your service so show respect to your students because they will market your business.
5. If you have a manual skill such as welding or spray painting offer a group of young men and women tuition, especially those who are unemployed, which will help them gain a skill to become productive and contributing members of society. You could get established businesses in your community to sponsor each candidate.

<u>Forecast</u>

If you work six days a week and you service four clients per day at R150 per client, you will earn R14400 per month. Not bad at all.

24. Ten Minute-Portrait Sketches

You would need to have a talent or skill in sketching. Just about every person is fascinated with themselves and sketching a person in ten minutes will add to the fascination of this business.

Outlay

1. Sketch pad/paper
2. Easel or large hard board
3. Pencils
4. Two chairs
5. Large double sided advertising board

How, What, Where, When, Who

1. Artists usually take weeks and months to complete a painting or artwork. You only take ten minutes. This is where people are going to be intrigued by your ability.
2. Seeing a sketch from start to finish in ten minutes is going to wow crowds.
3. Tell your friends and family about your service and encourage them to show your completed work to their friends and family.
4. Position yourself in shopping malls where you will be visible by crowds of people. Ensure that you have a double sided advertising board so that people can see from all angles while you are sketching. You do not want to stop sketching in order to explain your services as this will waste time.
5. Advertise your services at parties where there are many potential customers.

6. Sketch a portrait of someone from a photograph – people can give the portrait as a gift to the photographed person.
7. Give your business card along with the completed sketch so that potential customers know how and where to contact you.

X-Factor: <u>What makes your business different?</u>

1. Production time of ten minutes makes this a very unique business.
2. Allowing people to witness the product from start to finish fascinates them.
3. Draw three sketches where you age the customer. So you will draw the customer as young, then middle aged and then as an old person. Ask your customer if they smoke. We all know that smoking ages you so you can make them look extra old.
4. When your customer sees what they would potentially look like when they are old, this would surely be an incentive for them to stop smoking.
5. If you are drawing a thin young person, show them as fat person when they are older. This could also motivate people to take care of their diets.
6. Provide the correct sized frames for your sketches for an extra sum.

<u>Forecast</u>

If you charge R50 for a ten minute sketch and you sketch four people in an hour and you only work four hours a day for six days a week you will make R19 200 per month. Add the money from the sale of the frames and you are well on your way.

25. Home Makeovers

Many people live in homes where they never change the position of the furniture or freshen up the curtains. Very often we are so used to seeing untidy, dirty or shabby home interiors that we become oblivious to it. A home makeover need not cost much money.

Outlay

1. Paint
2. Network of appliance, furniture and home accessory providers

How, What, Where, When, Who

1. Most people need a home makeover but the first thing that they would say is that they cannot afford it.
2. Your business is about providing this service even if people have no money.
3. For the thrifty home makeover, all you have to do is shift the furniture around so that it gives the impression that something new has been introduced or so that a noticeable change is visible.
4. Shift cupboards and beds and clean up thoroughly.
5. Wash curtains and shift curtains to different rooms.
6. Paint old furniture.
7. Remove stained old carpets and varnish or paint floors
8. Sell unwanted items and purchase different items from charity shops or junk shops.

X-Factor: <u>What makes your business different?</u>

1. The service you offer is affordable to everyone. It is amazing how a house can look after a major clean-up and by just moving the furniture around.
2. You will cater to the pockets of individuals. Obviously if someone can afford to do more then you will comply with their request.
3. Bring in subtle changes like flowers or greenery from the garden and candles.
4. Use existing items in a recycled manner, e.g. turn an old vase into a lampshade stand, an old shoe becomes a plant holder etc.
5. Offer to makeover the garden or yard and use old junk in an attention-grabbing way, e.g. an old discarded toilet can be used as a pot plant holder, grow herbs in an old bath etc.
6. Increase the flow of energy by bringing more light into a room.
7. Start by making over your own home. Show your friends and family and ask them if you can makeover their homes.
8. Do a makeover in one day. This will surprise people but you will need the help of another person to move the furniture and to clean up.

<u>Forecast</u>

If you makeover two houses a week and you charge a R1000 per makeover, you will earn R8000 per month. This can of course be increased with more clients and by offering something extra such as new towels, candles or perhaps by baking a fresh loaf of bread in the clients house so that when they step into their newly made over house they are greeted with the smell of freshly baked bread. This is a technique that plays on the senses of the client.

26. Public/Motivational Speaker

A motivational speaker motivates and inspires people to take up a cause, become more productive in the workplace or take action in their personal lives. Motivational speaking is such a wide field and can include topics on spirituality, sport, business, personal development, the environment, social ills, politics etc. A motivational speaker must believe in what they do. You must have passion for what you do and in fact you must eat, sleep and breathe what you preach. A motivational speaker has highly developed coping strategies to deal with nerves and stage fright.

Outlay

1. A strong animated voice
2. A good sense of humour
3. Being able to think on your feet (note that non of these cost anything)

How, What, Where, When, Who

1. Decide on the area that you would like to speak on.
2. Subscribe to an annual motivational speakers or business directory.
3. Educate yourself on becoming a professional motivational speaker.
4. Ensure that your talks are interactive and visual, so provide visuals.
5. If it is not possible for you to provide visuals then you must become the visual, so ACT!
6. Make use of the most important instrument you have, your voice!

7. Advertise yourself to corporate and government wellness programmes. Remember schools and private functions too.
8. Create a website of your services so that the public knows what you offer and where they can contact you.
9. Brand your image by creating an illusion about yourself; you could be the joker, the glamorous diva, the 'bling-bling' guy, the sporty person, the impersonator, he who relates well to the youth, the exotic gay guy, the voluptuous madam etc.

X-Factor: <u>What makes your business different?</u>

1. Never turn down business, no matter how little it pays or where its location.
2. Create publicity for yourself and remember that there is no such thing as bad publicity. So call the media whenever you speak to a group and ask them to document the event.
3. Use social media networks to speak about your work (Twitter, Facebook, Email etc.)
4. Collaborate with an established motivational speaker on one or two events and learn from them. This is called piggybacking off someone's success or reputation. Remember to do the same for the new kid on the block once you are successful and well known.
5. Create your own blog so that you have followers who give you feedback and ideas about your service.

<u>Forecast</u>

Until you are more established your fee for various events may differ but at the beginning, let's say your fee is R2000 per event and you have two events per week, you could earn R8000. However with more experience come more publicity and more demand for your skills.

27. Designer Skincare and Hair Care Products

Design your own skincare and hair care products. There are hundreds of recipes on the internet or perhaps you already have a tried and tested recipe from a family member. Everybody washes their hair regularly and at least one in five people have a hair or skin problem. This business is about research, educating yourself and experimentation.

Outlay

1. Ingredients
2. Mixing bowls
3. Measuring cups and spoons
4. Jars and dispensers
5. Labels

How, What, Where, When, Who

1. Every hair and skin product has a base. Decide what kind of base you want to use. Vegetable or fruit oil base, chemical, tree oil, seed/nut oil base.
2. Educate yourself on the dangers of using certain products as you do not want your customers to get skin or hair damage as this could damage your reputation and your business may suffer.
3. Use oils such as Argan and Jojoba oil, they have healing properties for skin and hair.
4. Investigate which aromatherapy oils you could add to your base.
5. Create liquid soap for hands and bodies; especially for sports people.
6. Decide which packaging will be best for your product. Some products become damaged if stored in plastic or clear glass.

Investigate the uses of porcelain, baked clay and dark glass as a packaging option.
7. Ensure that you have smaller tubs you can use for samples.
8. Eczema and acne are such common conditions and many sufferers find minimum relief from topical creams so perhaps you will stumble onto a natural ingredient that works wonders for such conditions.
9. It is very important to get feedback from your customers. Value their experiences of your product as it is the only way you will improve your product.
10. Host parties for your friends and family where they experiment with your products.
11. Host workshops where you talk about natural oils and ingredients and get your customers to experiment mixing their own hair and skin ingredients. Give each customer two tubs to store their hair and skin concoctions.
12. Sell a hair care product and add a skincare sample as a gift. Ask for feedback on the sample.
13. Add a small brochure about your business concept, and a hair or skin success story. This becomes a great marketing tool as the story starts to spread.
14. Ensure that your products cover a range of hair and skin conditions, e.g. oily and dry hair and skin, eczema and acne, dandruff etc.

X-Factor: <u>What makes your business different?</u>

1. The fact that you use fresh and high quality ingredients.
2. Your openness and receptivity to customer feedback.
3. Your willingness to improve your products.
4. Your willingness to design special products for special customers and their individual conditions.
5. Design a special ointment for pain or inflammation or for psoriasis.

6. Investigate the use of indigenous plant material.
7. Your designer packaging and your designer label.
8. Your own network marketing. Get customers to buy in bulk from you and to sell at a higher price so that they are empowered to start their own businesses.

Forecast

If you work five days a week and sell four tubs of skin cream and four tubs of hair care products at R25 a tub daily, you will make R4000. Remember you will make more money from your network marketing bulk sales as well as from your workshops and special customers.

28. The Colonial Tea Room

The tea room or tea shop is a largely untapped market in this country. Most areas have coffee shops but the tea room is almost unheard of. There are so many refreshing brands of tea that can be sourced from all over the world and this is a wonderful way to educate your customer.

Outlay

1. Crockery and cutlery
2. Tea trays
3. Teapots and tea cosy's
4. Tea and sugar
5. Cakes and sandwiches
6. Rental for venue
7. Staff salaries

How, What, Where, When, Who

1. Educate yourself on the different brands of tea grown all over the world. You can choose to do internet research and also travel to tea growing countries such as India, China, Kenya, South Africa and certain South American countries.
2. Tea can be used for refreshing and quenching purposes but there are also teas that are used for medicinal and health purposes. Such as detoxing teas, tea that increases the metabolism, slimming teas, sleep teas, digestion teas etc.
3. During the colonial era tea rooms were very fashionable. You can bring that fashion back with colonial décor and colonial styled teapots and crockery.
4. People love history and stories about the past so incorporate some colonial or historical events into your tea room concept.

5. Watch some 1920 and 1930 movies to get an idea of what was fashionable during the colonial period.
6. Serve only two cakes, e.g. scones with jam and cream and crumpets. However serve an array of sandwiches. The sandwich was very fashionable during the colonial era. Do not have an extravagant menu as this will only push up your costs.
7. Offer tea leaf readings. Once a customer has drunk their tea you will swirl their tea cup and read the leaves at the bottom of the cup. This is a skill that you can learn. This was very common and popular during colonial times.
8. At a later stage when your business is more established you could acquire an "olden days" car and fetch and transport customers in the local vicinity.

X-Factor: <u>What makes your business different?</u>

1. People will pay money to come and experience this concept.
2. Give your customers the option of buying tea leaves in packages. You can add a small brochure and leaflet advertising your business as well as where the tea was grown.
3. You can also become a supplier of bulk tea to other establishments.
4. Tea leaf readings will become very trendy.
5. If you decide to travel to tea growing countries document your travels and video the tea picking process. Put this short documentary on your website so people can see the process of tea leaf picking to tea leaf drying to tea in the teapot.
6. Remember the fashionable tea cosy! You could also sell unusual teapots.
7. Drink your tea with your pinkie finger raised…very fashionable! This can become the trademark of your business.
8. Encourage your customers to use your venue for tea parties, baby showers and birthday parties.

9. Remember to stay in touch with your customer by asking them what they liked or did not enjoy about their experience. Use this information to improve your business.
10. If at first you cannot afford to rent premises, use an old caravan and take your business to your customer.

Forecast

If your establishment is open six days a week and you sell 20 cups of tea per day at R15 per cup (tea reading included) and 10 scones at R10 each plus 10 sandwiches at R15 each you will make R13 200 per month. Remember that you will make extra money from selling tea packages to your customers as well as to your suppliers and other businesses.

29. Shoes for Sore Feet

At least one in five people suffer from some kind of feet discomfort. Feet problems range from bunions, calluses, flat feet, corns, corrective surgery issues, claw toes, corns and generally tired and sore feet. Design a shoe or range of shoes that accommodates and resolves almost all of these problems.

Outlay

1. Machinery
2. Leather and accessories
3. Shoe boxes

How, What, Where, When, Who

1. There are two parts to this business. The one part is designing a shoe that resolves or relieves almost all of the issues that cause or aggravate pain in the feet. The other part of this business is to design a fashionable shoe that appeals to all across the board.
2. The bottom or sole section of the shoe needs to be constructed from a material that acts as a shock absorber to the foot.
3. The design of the human foot needs to be re-examined because shoes are not designed to accommodate the flexible walking movement of the foot.
4. Designing the top covering of the shoe is a much easier and more creative process.
5. The human foot is not designed to be able to walk comfortably on shoes that are more than four centimetres in height.
6. Heels that are too high inevitably affect the tendons in the foot and shorten the muscles in the calves not to mention the

damage caused by the pressure placed on the knees, hips and lower back.

7. Most business ideas are born out of a problem that needs a solution. This is a huge market that begs for a solution to the problem.
8. The male shoe market also needs a healthy alternative to fashion. In terms of health shoes for males, this is a largely untapped market.
9. Advertise your product twice a month in local newspapers (middle of the month for government employees and end of the month for other consumers)
10. Create a website where you display your product. Give your customers the option of purchasing online.
11. Give discounts on bulk purchases.
12. Sell your product to high end retail stores.
13. Create an exclusive label or brand name for your product.
14. Source materials from third world countries at cost price. Investigate the use of materials that 'breathe' better.

X-Factor: <u>What makes your business different?</u>

1. You have the solution to a problem that the consumer has been begging for.
2. Your product is unique. The same product cannot be found in any other shoe store.
3. The customer has different means of accessing your product.
4. The customer does not have to compromise fashion for comfort. They are getting both in one form.
5. There are shoe seats in your store so that the customer can sit and fit on their shoes. You assist the customer to fit on the shoes. This is a non existent service nowadays. Shoe sales staff never assists the customer to fit on their shoes. This practice died in the late 1970's to early 1980's. Such a

pity…Nowadays the customer is lucky if the shoe store has a chair to sit on.

Forecast

If you work six days a week and sell four pairs of shoes per day at R200 per pair, you will make R19 200 per month. Remember that you will make more money from your online sales as well as your bulk sales.

30. Dream Big

This is a business where you show others how to dream big. Many people can only think as far as their own experiences will allow them. The target group for this business would be youth from disadvantaged communities. Even though we live in such a technologically advanced era we still have young people who think that having a child and getting married is the ultimate in life. Dream big and you can make anything possible. But how do you dream big if you do not know what the possibilities are?

<u>Outlay</u>

1. A vehicle to get from point A to point B
2. A telephone or cellular phone
3. A computer with Internet access
4. A wide network of contacts

<u>How, What, Where, When, Who</u>

1. How do you dream big? Remember that big dreams are not only about money. Big dreams are about history, geographical locations, inventions, manufacturing, entertainment, travel, different cultures, ancient belief systems, sport, education etc.
2. Teach young people about all of the above. How? Make your teaching interactive and visual. Make use of the experiences of heroes and role models. Host competitions, exercises, programmes, assignments, research, travel opportunities, interaction with others who have dreamt big etc.
3. Your target market will be schools, township communities, low income groups as well as very talented individuals.

Target young people who have a small dream and help them develop it into a big dream.

4. Get government to buy into your programme. Speak to the media about your concept. Get sponsorship and donors from local and overseas businesses and organizations.
5. Use your persuasive skills to get volunteers and helpers on board. Once your organization grows you can begin to employ people. Dream big yourself and take this organization outside of the South African (or your own country's) borders.

X-Factor: What makes your business different?

1. Your target market is a group of people who are young and impressionable. You can impress upon them the ability to change their thought patterns and to see the world differently.
2. This business will have massive positive spin offs to combat teen pregnancies and drug abuse. You are giving young people something positive to hold onto.
3. You help these young people to find sponsorship to catapult them into their big dream.
4. Not only do you target youth but you target adults who have not had similar opportunities and who feel that they have missed out. There is something so rewarding about helping an older person achieve their dream.
5. Use the success stories generated from this business to influence more young people and to gain more sponsorship.
6. Help young and old with life coaching and career guidance. Steer them into the right job direction that will catapult them into their big dream.

Forecast

It is not easy to forecast the monetary aspect of this business but this business can very easily become an institution in the South African (or your own country's) context. The dream big business can become the next port of call for almost every young and older person.

31. Adoption/Missing Person's Tracer

An adoption tracer or missing person's tracer can be a very rewarding business. There are many biological parents who have given up their children for adoption due to circumstances and are now seeking their biological children. There are many adopted children who are seeking their biological parents for closure or for whatever reason. Similarly, many people go missing and their families endure immense trauma not knowing where their loved ones are.

Outlay

1. A telephone and cellular phone
2. A computer with Internet access

How, What, Where, When, Who

1. This business requires someone with intuitive skills and common sense. You also need to have a plan of action as to where to begin your search.
2. You will need details of the person that you are searching, e.g. date of birth, identity number, last known location, financial records, friends and places of work, hospital records, social media networks, photograph, archival records etc.
3. Most of your work will be done via the computer and telephone. Research how to become a tracer of missing persons as there is a load of information on this subject. Also research what the fee structure for this business should be. This also depends on the location and socio-economic class of your client.
4. Once you have located the person that you are searching for, establish a communication link between the missing person

and the family before the initial contact meeting. This is important as either party will have expectations and may very well be disappointed if their expectations are not met.
5. Advertise your services at established adoption agencies, state welfare agencies, newspapers, social media networks, police stations, retail stores and your website.

X-Factor: <u>What makes your business different?</u>

1. Your success rate at finding people. So work hard on your reputation.
2. Bringing people together and helping them to find closure.
3. Your business has a face and a person behind the telephone so make face to face contact with your client.
4. You can also trace people who are in debt and have absconded.
5. Do not make promises that you cannot keep.
6. You have established international networks for yourself so you know how to find people not living in South Africa (or your own country).
7. Start an adoption/missing persons online register where people pay to become a member. Here they will register their information if they are looking for someone and this information becomes accessible for someone looking for that person, i.e. both parties register and so the database is built up.
8. Your ability to solve cold cases.
9. Genealogy and family trees. You are able to help people trace their roots and bloodline. This helps to bring families together. Perhaps inheritances can be claimed. Lost relatives can also be found this way.

Forecast

Find out what the going rate is and peg your fee at a similar structure. Charge more if you have to travel or make international calls. You will grow your detective and intuitive abilities and this can be so gratifying.

32. Finishing School

Many young boys and girls are not getting the guidance from their parents, schools, society and peers that they require in order to become independent productive citizens. We live in such a fast paced technological environment that most of these institutions cannot maintain the technological pace. We tend to spend our time trying to keep up technologically but we have completely neglected the rites of passage pertaining to young boys and girls.

Outlay

1. A telephone and cellular phone
2. A computer with Internet access
3. A network of contacts

How, What, Where, When, Who

1. What is a rite of passage and what is its function? A rite of passage is an event which marks the transition and entry from one stage to another. The function of a rite of passage is to ensure that an initiate emerges with a new identity.
2. Common rites of passage include First Holy Communion, Confirmation, Bar Mitzvahs, 21st Birthdays, Engagements, Marriage and Death. However, in many instances these rites of passage are underplayed and are becoming less popular.
3. Young people are now creating their own rites of passage, which include extracting their front teeth, losing their virginity, getting tattoos and piercings, having children, smoking cigarettes or experimenting with drugs etc.
4. Finishing school marks milestones in a young person's life and prepares them for the next level/stage.

5. Creating positive rites of passage such as finding a part time job and learning the value of independence and earning your own money while still at school, learning life skills that are going to help you in adult life, e.g. public speaking, interview skills, self defence skills, dating/courting and relationship skills, self esteem and confidence building skills, social and etiquette skills, health and hygiene, first aid, deportment and make-up etc.
6. You can host one-year programmes, weekend programmes, holiday programmes and evening classes.
7. Advertise your finishing school at schools, workplaces, education departments, welfare organization and through the Internet.
8. Influence parents to support their children in becoming well rounded adults.

X-Factor: What makes your business different?

1. Invite guest speakers who are heroes and role models to young people.
2. Target boys and girls but host separate classes for both groups.
3. Target older or more mature adults for your evening classes.
4. Invite your successful candidates back to share their experiences with the new groups.
5. Get the parents involved.
6. Teach young people to raise their standards.
7. Teach young people to love and respect themselves first.
8. Host ceremonies where parents can witness a rite of passage that their child has gone through.

<u>Forecast</u>

This type of business can become an institution and a beacon of hope in the community. Your success is shown in the number of young people who become upstanding citizens and who plough back into their families and communities. The possibilities for earning money are endless but you have to carry this vision forward with a very high standard.

33. Landscape Gardening

This business would require someone with a love for the outdoors and specifically a love of gardening. You will need to have prior knowledge and information about landscaping but you can also teach yourself these skills through classes and through research.

Outlay

1. Labour
2. A vehicle
3. Gardening equipment
4. Potting soil and various plant foods
5. Plants

How, What, Where, When, Who

1. Focus on all sized gardens including balconies for those who live in flats or complexes.
2. You will need a few helpers to ensure that the job is done in the shortest possible time.
3. Know where to source the most cost effective materials and supplies.
4. Make sure that you use seasonal plants and inform your clients that plants do not live forever and that they need to be fed.
5. Offer your services to maintain the landscaped garden afterwards.
6. Ask your customers to refer you to their families and friends. Take before and after photographs and ask local newspapers and free magazines to showcase your work. Remember to give people your business card or contact details.

7. Remember the corporate market, e.g. hotels, guest houses, business balconies, spas and lodges etc.
8. There is no job too big or too small for you.
9. Offer high quality service to all even if your client is poor or disadvantaged. Remember word gets around.

X-Factor: <u>What makes your business different?</u>

1. Offer themed landscaped gardens, e.g. low maintenance pebbled gardens, pot plant gardens, aloe and cactus gardens, water gardens, Zen gardens, bonsai gardens, lawns, tree gardens, indigenous gardens, fruit gardens, vegetable gardens, hedge maze, herb gardens, miniature forests, rooftop gardens etc.
2. Use feng shui or geometrical principles to design your gardens.
3. Designing and building labyrinths in gardens and on rooftop gardens to aid in the alleviation of stress.
4. Roof gardens of complexes and apartment buildings.
5. Teach your clients about how to care for their plants.
6. Offer an aftercare service.
7. The shortest amount of time in which you take to complete a garden. Make sure that you have the labour and equipment to keep this promise.
8. Put signage on your vehicle so that potential clients can see your business name and contact telephone number.

<u>Forecast</u>

You will have to do a costing of the square meterage of the garden area as well as the cost of the plants and other gardening material. This business is labour intensive but can yield huge profits and adds to the beauty and well being of our planet.

34. Ecosystem Gardening

Ecosystems beautify and aid our environment in all kinds of ways. This is a largely untapped business and the benefits for the environment are many. The human population has interfered with and aided in the destruction of almost every ecosystem on the planet. An ecosystem is a smaller version of a biome. A biome is a large area of vegetation that depends on the climate to sustain it, i.e. the Amazon rainforest and the Sahara desert are biomes. An ecosystem is a smaller version of a biome, i.e. you can have a flourishing ecosystem in your garden, in a fish tank or in a bottle. Ecosystems invite all kinds of wildlife into your garden, e.g. frogs, snails, butterflies, birds, dragon flies, bees, spiders, ants and various insects.

Outlay

1. Wood, soil, sand or water
2. Gardening equipment
3. Plants
4. Plant food, e.g. manure, bone meal, mulch and compost

How, What, Where, When, Who

1. You need to have knowledge and information about various ecosystems, e.g. aquatic, woodland and desert ecosystems are the common ones. Someone who has a conservation or biology background would do well in this business.
2. If you have no prior knowledge or skills in this field you can still learn by educating yourself. Do Internet research and visit Carole Sevilla Brown's Ecosystem gardening website. She also has a free e-newsletter where she teaches

prospective gardening enthusiasts about ecosystem gardening.

3. You can advertise your services to private homes, the municipality (parks and open spaces), schools, farms, spas and guest houses etc.

4. Remember that for ecosystem gardening you would have to use organic gardening material as herbicides, pesticides and fertilizers will kill wildlife.

5. Take photographs of your completed ecosystem gardens and ask the owners of these gardens to write a short paragraph on what they feel about their new ecosystem gardens.

6. Add this information to your website and post it online so that other gardening enthusiasts become interested in your product and concept.

7. Ask various media companies to publish your photographs and information so that you can get free publicity.

X-factor: <u>What makes your business different?</u>

1. You are providing and replenishing the planet with a home for its wildlife.

2. You now have the ability to educate others about the value of having an ecosystem garden in their backyard.

3. An ecosystem garden at a school provides valuable education for school children. Children will see and learn from nature instead of from a text book only.

4. Every individual who has an ecosystem garden will learn about the energy pyramid and its food chain and how the network of relations between organism and the ecosystem influences one another.

5. Ecosystem gardens can also be built indoors so educate yourself on how to do this and market your concept to those who live in complexes, flats and to individuals who simply want to bring nature into the home.

Forecast

If you do three ecosystem gardens a week, i.e. a small, medium and large one and you charge R1000, R3000 and R5000 respectively, you will earn R9000 per week, which translates to R36 000 per month. Of course you will need to do proper costing of your materials and labour but overall this could be a very lucrative and rewarding business venture.

35. Burglar Bars and Security Gates

There is always a need for this kind of business but you will certainly have to have a flair for design and you will also need to update your knowledge on what is current and fashionable. You will need to be skilled as a welder but if you aren't then attend a welding course at a technical college in order to gain this skill. You will also need to have knowledge of mathematics especially geometry as most of the designs of burglar bars and security gates are geometric shapes.

Outlay

1. A welding machine
2. Welding rods
3. Steel rods
4. Metal primer and galvanising paint
5. A drill

How, What, Where, When, Who

1. Burglar bars can be inserted into walls using drills and cement or they can be screwed onto the window frame.
2. Your market will include the corporate market; most businesses need security. So do schools and private homes.
3. Advertise your services at hardware stores, home décor and appliance stores and home and hardware magazines and remember that there are many magazines and newspapers that allow small businesses to advertise for free.
4. Remember to advertise by word of mouth and ask your customers to tell their friends and family about your business.
5. For every referral you could offer a gift. People love receiving gifts as acknowledgement of their efforts and it does not have to be expensive.

X-factor: <u>What makes your business different?</u>

1. Find the client instead of the client finding you. Walk down each street in your community with pictures/portfolio of your product and designs. Target homes and businesses that do not have burglar bars and security gates.
2. Remember to sign a contract with your customer before you begin a job and also remember to take a 50% deposit before you commence with a job because if a customer disappoints you, at least your costs will be covered. By signing a contract with your customer and by taking a 50% deposit you will be conducting your business in a professional manner.
3. Remember to advise your customers on the best designs and the safest steel rods to use for their gates.
4. Ask your customers if they have pets and design your steel gates in such a way that small pets cannot or can climb through the bars. Most often customers do not think about these details and only realize this when it is too late.
5. You could add spikes to the top of walls and gates as an extra safety measure.

<u>Forecast</u>

If you do two small jobs per week, at R1000 each and two large jobs per week at R4000 each; you will earn R40 000 per month. Not bad.

36. Dog Training

Dog training can be such a fun job because you are almost always outdoors. This business requires you to have patience and an understanding of dog behaviour. If you do not understand animal behaviour then you can complete an animal communication course where you will learn to communicate with animals on an intuitive level.

Outlay

1. Leashes (three different sizes)
2. Hoops and balls
3. A whistle

How, What, Where, When, Who

1. Remember that dogs do not understand right and wrong behaviour. They only understand safe and dangerous behaviour.
2. Project yourself into the animal kingdom and observe how animals behave. Do not try and project human behaviour and social skills onto animals. Once you start observing animal behaviour, you will come to understand that they communicate just like children who cannot speak properly.
3. Animals have similar needs to children. They need to feel safe, they thrive on lots of love, affection and praise, they need a healthy diet, and they need exercise and time for fun and play.
4. Puppies are in fact babies. They learn by repetition and by exploring. While you are teaching a puppy they may be distracted by some noise or object and forget what you have just taught them. Remember not to shout and become

impatient as you will damage your pups confidence and nervous system.

5. Design pamphlets of your services and advertise your business at dog grooming parlours, veterinaries, animal shelters etc.
6. Find out where and how police and tracker dogs are trained and investigate these skills.
7. Attend dog shows and become acquainted with pet owners and their needs and incorporate these into your business.

X-Factor: What makes your business different?

1. Your understanding, compassion and love for animals will make their owners feel safe with you.
2. Your dog training methods will be fun so your dog clients will learn very quickly because they will enjoy what you are teaching them.
3. You specialize in "bad" behaviour so you know how to re-socialize dogs.
4. You teach pet owners how to exercise their dogs. Owners also get a work-out by roller blading, cycling and running with their pets alongside them.

Forecast

If you train two dogs per day at R100 per session and you work six days per week you will earn R4800 per month. As your training techniques become more popular you will increase your clientele and with more experience you can even add animal communication to your package.

37. Talent Scout

This can be such a rewarding business. You will however need to have an eye for spotting talent as well as persuasive skills. In many instances the best talents and the roughest diamonds are found in the poorest communities. These children and adults are extremely resilient because of the challenging paths they have walked.

Outlay

1. A vehicle
2. A telephone and cellular phone
3. A computer with Internet access
4. A network of contacts

How, What, Where, When, Who

1. Where will you find your future stars? In your own community of course! Attend school swimming galas, school concerts, community festivals and shows, school sporting events and soccer, rugby and cricket tournaments.
2. Start compiling a network of people who can catapult your potential stars into prominence.
3. Become acquainted with people who work for the media so that you can get media coverage on your potential star.
4. Get local and big business involved in your endeavour to sponsor and support local talent.
5. Team up with local and international celebrities and ask if they will share a stage or showcase these young potential stars at their shows.
6. Create an event where a percentage of the proceeds are donated to a good cause in your town or city. This also gives

the potential stars exposure which will catapult them onto a stage, platform etc.

7. Find endorsements and sponsorships for young talents.
8. Encourage your potential talents to participate in all established events such as big walks, cycling events, modelling, charity drives and invite the media to cover these events. Remember that the more exposure you get the more people with money will come to notice these young talents.
9. There is no event too big or too small (as long as it is legal) that your future talent cannot participate in.
10. Your potential star will not be paying you but you will get endorsements from big companies, sponsorship from sport companies and organizations, competitions, advertising and payment when your star piggybacks off another star or event.
11. What are the areas that catapult talented individuals into prominence? They are sport, acting, singing, modelling, music, dance, science, comedy etc.

X-Factor: <u>What makes your business different?</u>

1. You have your future talent's best interests at heart. Know when to let go.
2. Give guidance about the dangers of the limelight, e.g. drugs, alcohol, leeches and mooches.
3. Always involve the parents of the potential star if he/she is under age. Encourage parents to attend these events even if the child has reached the age of majority. Talented children flourish when they are supported.
4. Know when to push and encourage and know when to step back to allow the potential star to learn from their own mistakes.
5. Do not abuse your power! If you do, you will eventually be the loser. Remember that with power comes responsibility so I remind you to know when to step back.

Forecast

Money from this business is usually seen over time. You need to develop relationships with your potential stars as well as their sponsors. You would normally take a commission or percentage of what is earned but this has to be contractually agreed upon early in the relationship. Remember that your potential stars will not stay with you forever. They will eventually move on and make room for new talent, so know when to let go.

38. T-shirt Design

This is already a very well known business but can still be extremely creative and lucrative. The T-shirt has been in fashion for decades and seems will never go out of fashion. If you don't know how to design a T-shirt you can research the free tutorials on the Internet which give you the step-by-step process.

Outlay

1. White T-shirts
2. A computer with appropriate software
3. A steam iron
4. A scanner

How, What, Where, When, Who

1. Firstly you will need to source inexpensive good quality T-shirts. Go with white at the beginning as this could be your cheaper option.
2. You will need a computer with a good programme such as Photoshop but you can research other options.
3. You will need a good quality steam iron and later you can buy an industrial steam iron.
4. You can create your own drawings and designs, scan them into your computer and use Photoshop to enhance or exaggerate your design.
5. Ensure that you follow the news and whoever is in the news, download their pictures and Photoshop to suit your needs. Follow the popular culture because there are always fads and people want what is in fashion.
6. So track big concerts, conferences, business summits, big walks, sporting events, fashion and modelling shows,

competitions such as Miss SA or Miss World/Universe, Miss Gay Pride, religious events etc and sell T-shirts with these events, logo's and faces printed on them.

7. Tap into certain markets like teeny boppers, the geek market, and computer game market and take note of what their interests are.

8. Take note of celebrations such as St Valentine's Day and religious celebrations. Also take note of political rallies, protest marches and strikes as this can also be a lucrative market because of the numbers of people who would want to be associated with such events.

X-Factor: <u>What makes your business different?</u>

1. Your interest and knowledge of current affairs gives you the edge over your competitors.

2. You advertise to large markets of people, i.e. schools, rallies, marches, big walks etc.

3. Expand your interest and knowledge to international current affairs. Remember that there are many foreign nationals living in every country.

4. Expand your sales to foreign markets such as China, India, South America, Europe etc.

5. You could write poetry, jokes and lyrics of songs on your T-shirts.

6. Foreign sales will require you to be au fait with online purchasing and payment and you would need to set up a website and maintain it with your latest designs

7. You could also do designs that are requested. Your designs could also be sold to companies for royalties and this would save you the trouble of having to make T-shirts.

Forecast

If you sell four T-shirts a day for R50 per T-shirt and you work six days per week you will make R4800 per month. Remember you could earn a lot more from your bulk sales and your foreign sales, not to mention your royalties from T-shirt designs.

39. Fashion Stylist

This is a creative and fashion orientated business and you will always be surrounded by ideas, colour and texture. This business has many facets; you can work from home, travel or operate from a retail clothing store. You will need to have a very bubbly personality in order to excite and engage your clients.

Outlay

1. A cellular phone

How, What, Where, When, Who

1. You will have to have a flair for clothing, fashion, design, fabric texture, colour combination, accessories and style.
2. You could operate from your own business (home or commercial). You could also operate from a clothing store.
3. You could sell your services to fashion shows and big modelling events.
4. You could sell your services to film companies and drama/concert shows, however, you must have knowledge of period costume and historical dress codes.
5. Most men and women do not know how to accessorize their garments nor do many people know how to dress for their body-types; this is where you lend your expertise.
6. You could offer workshops on how to dress and accessorize without buying too many clothing items. Know what the basic clothes are that you should have in your wardrobe.

X-Factor: What makes your business different?

1. Teach your customer to recycle their clothing and save money.
2. Teach your customer to combine fabric textures to create a wow look.
3. Teach your customer how to create a vintage, Goth or theme look.
4. Advise your clients what to do with outdated and old clothing.
5. You will go on shopping expeditions with your clients and offer advice.
6. You can offer your services to high end fashion stores on certain days and earn extra cash for helping their clients. Leave your contact details with the store manager and let them know that you can help their customers to make wise purchases; the store can only benefit from this.
7. Teach your clients where to hunt for bargains.
8. You could add tips for make-up and shoes to your services.

Forecast:

If you work six days per week and service two clients per day and are paid R250 per client, you will earn R12 000 per month. If you host one workshop per month at R3000 and assist at shows for a further R2000 per month you will earn a total of R17 000 per month - not to mention the other extras.

40. Fairy Light Decorations

Hanging up fairy lights around homes can look so enchanting. This business requires you to have knowledge of electricity and electrical connections. You will need to invest in a large number of fairy lights, which you will decorate around your client's house for a limited period of time then you will go and remove them.

Outlay

1. Fairy lights
2. Electrical cables
3. Extension cords and plugs

How, What, Where, When, Who

1. Purchase a large number of fairy lights. Do not invest in colour lights yet as they are too expensive.
2. You need to have an idea of how you are going to hang these lights around the house. Think of various designs and research how fairy lights are hung and the patterns that are used.
3. Advertise your services for birthdays, especially for children, weddings, and welcome home events, Christmas, religious festivals and all special occasions.
4. Market your services at toy shops, party shops, in free home décor magazines and hardware stores etc.
5. Create a website of pictures with all your fairy light decorations.
6. Remember to ask your clients for referrals.

X-Factor: <u>What makes your business different?</u>

1. You create a fantasy world for the client.
2. You install and remove the fairy light decorations so the client has absolutely no work to do.
3. The same lights are used over and over, thus the business becomes more and more cost effective over time.

<u>Forecast</u>

If you decorate two homes per week at R500 per home you will earn R4000 per month. Remember that your business will escalate during peak seasons when more people have extra money to spend.

41. Photographer and Videographer

People are always looking for professional photographers and videographers. You would need to have a qualification or proven experience for this business. Do research on well known photographers and the type of photos that made them famous.

<u>Outlay</u>

1. A good quality camera
2. A good quality video camera (optional)

<u>How, What, Where, When, Who</u>

1. Get a good quality digital camera and or video camera.
2. Take pictures of babies. Keep servicing the parent as the baby grows older. So keep in touch with your client and make courtesy calls.
3. Take before and after pictures of people, homes, cars etc. as they perform make-over projects on these things.
4. Many young men and women want to create their own modelling portfolios. You can also advertise your services at professional modelling agencies.
5. Nowadays it is also very popular to have a video taken of a wedding or a funeral. People want to have all kinds of keepsakes and memories.
6. Car shows, big walks, graduations, school concerts, sport events and news making events etc.
7. You can also take pictures of nature, e.g. sunsets and animals and sell them to nature magazines
8. Sell your pictures to travel, fashion, home décor magazines and newspapers.

9. Market your services by dropping brochures with funeral parlours, churches, caterers, event management companies etc.
10. Photographing food for food magazines can also be very lucrative.

X-factor: <u>What makes your business different?</u>

1. Bring photography to your client. Make yourself visible. Do not wait for your client to find you.
2. Make sure that you host regular displays and exhibitions of your work.
3. You can host informal and formal exhibitions, i.e. in school halls and foyers, in business foyers and lounges, in shopping malls, in museums, in subways, stations, airports and parks where many commuters are found.
4. Photograph township life and how people live.
5. The idea is to bring your work to life so that everybody can enjoy and experience what your camera sees.
6. Take ID photographs for drivers' licences, passports and identity (ID) documents. In fact you could get a shipping container as your 'shop' and just focus on this aspect of the business.

<u>Forecast</u>

If you photograph two events per week and you earn R1000 for each, you will make R 8000 per month. This business requires you to be proactive so you need to find events and people that you can photograph every day. You could also make a lot more money by taking ID photographs.

42. Grandma's Pantry

This is a business that has two features. The first feature is the part where you make your own homemade produce. The second feature is where you source homemade produce from other "Grannies Pantries".

Outlay

1. A hygienic kitchen
2. Packaging material
3. Ingredients

How, What, Where, When, Who

1. Create what people love but are too busy to make their own, e.g. homemade jams, pickles, biscuits, sweets, chocolates, stewed fruit, ginger beer, frozen pastry, etc.
2. Buy large quantities of tea and coffee and package them into smaller packets with your label attached.
3. Ensure that you make produce for special events such as Valentines Day, Easter and Christmas, e.g. heart chocolates, Christmas cakes and puddings and the famous pickled fish during Easter etc.
4. You can include everyday yummy treats if you have a good recipe, e.g. pies, quiches and cakes, fudge etc.
5. When your stock is running low you can source more homemade produce from your "Granny" suppliers.

X-Factor: What makes your business different?

1. Source your clients and take your business to their doorsteps.
2. Start by selling your products to your family and friends.

3. Make gift baskets because this allows one client to buy more than one product.
4. Sell your products and gift baskets to big businesses.
5. Remember to leave your contact details with your customers so that they can refer you and conduct repeat business with you.

Forecast

If you sell two gift baskets a week at R500 per gift basket, you will make R 4000 per month. Remember you will make extra sales from individual items and daily treats.

43. Gift Basket Business

This is such an easy yet creative business. Create gift baskets with themes as well as surprise gift baskets.

Outlay

1. Cellophane
2. Cello-tape
3. Wrapping paper
4. Ribbons
5. Your product

How, What, Where, When, Who

1. Source products from retail stores as well as from exclusive stores.
2. Create themed gift baskets, e.g. Valentine gift baskets, wedding gift baskets, baby shower gift baskets, pantry gift baskets, glassware gift baskets, toy gift baskets, soap, shower and shampoo gift baskets, shoe gift baskets, clothing and hair accessory gift baskets etc.
3. Ensure that you learn special skills in gift wrapping. You will need ribbon, wrapping paper, cellophane, tissue paper, glitter, wood shavings, hay, potpourri, newspaper etc.
4. Start by advertising your gift baskets to your friends and family. Showcase your gift baskets at markets and fares.
5. Take orders and ask your clients to give you a 50% deposit on the order.
6. Market your product to large businesses and remember that the more unusual the gift basket the more interest it will generate.

X-Factor: <u>What makes your business different?</u>

1. Opening one of your gift baskets is so exciting it invites the inner child in everyone to come and have fun.
2. Your gift baskets do not follow the norms and rules of gift giving.
3. Your gift wrapping is very beautiful yet unconventional.
4. You offer gift wrapping workshops.
5. Make smaller or miniature sized gift baskets at reduced prices.
6. Sell gift wrapping and accessories.

<u>Forecast</u>

If you sell one gift basket per day at R250 per basket and you work six days a week you will earn R6000 per month. Remember you will make extra money from your miniature gift baskets, gift wrapping workshops and gift wrapping and accessories.

44. Teach Craft Skills

This business requires the skills of a highly skilled crafter. You must really enjoy what you do and be extremely creative, patient and willing to share your talents with others in a safe and non threatening way.

Outlay

1. Craft material
2. A cellular phone

How, What, Where, When, Who

1. Crafts that you can teach are soap making, candle making, knitting, crocheting, quilt making, scrap booking, jewellery making, decoupage, art/painting etc.
2. Advertise your classes at community centres, in local newspapers, in craft magazines, craft shops, shopping malls, church groups, retirement homes, schools and amongst your family and friends.
3. Photograph the work of your students and post it on your website or social media site.
4. Invite conversation about your classes on social media sites as you may be inspired to change or offer variations of your skills.
5. Increase your class size during school holidays so make sure that you advertise at schools.

X-Factor: What makes your business different?

1. You are sharing your valuable skills and talents with others.

2. This encourages young and old alike at being creative, active with their minds and inspired to create projects for pleasure as well as for business purposes.
3. You can make a dying craft like knitting or crocheting become popular and in demand again.
4. By teaching your skills you get a class full of clients instead of one.
5. Painting/art can be used as a means of therapy.

Forecast

If you charge R50 for a class and you teach four people per day and you work five days a week you will earn R 4000 per month. The more people you speak to the more classes you will have so ask your former students to refer you to their friends and family.

45. Baby Sitting and Pet Sitting

Most families will have a child or a pet. Looking after someone else's child or pet can be gratifying especially because you will learn so much from a child or a pet.

Outlay

1. A cellular phone

How, What, Where, When, Who

1. Advertise your services amongst your friends and family, church groups, schools in your neighbourhood and at work if you have another job.
2. Ensure that you have basic first aid knowledge such as CPR (cardiopulmonary resuscitation) and the Heimlich manoeuvre (a precaution for choking).
3. When baby sitting, depending on the age of the child make your time with him/her as interactive as possible.
4. Teach a child to swim, dance, play a musical instrument or learn a language.
5. This can be done at a slow pace like learning five new words every time you baby sit the same child.
6. Teach a child to paint or draw and definitely read stories.
7. If you are looking after a pet ensure that you understand animal behaviour. Pets need to feel safe and loved. Do not threaten a pet by shouting or hitting them.
8. Teach a pet basic commands such as 'sit, stay, come, down'.
9. Teach a pet tricks like rolling over, jumping for a frisbee and playing catch with a ball etc.
10. If the pet you are looking after is very intelligent teach him/her more commands and speak to the pet with repetitive expressions but ensure that it is done in a fun and playful

way. Remember to reward the pet for good behaviour with doggy biscuits or treats.

X-Factor: What makes your business different?

1. The parent or owner of the child or pet will notice a visible positive difference in their child or pet.
2. Parents feel very proud when their children learn a new language or learn to play a musical instrument.
3. Parents will want your services because you offer something different.
4. Help children with homework and projects. This will be a great help to the parent.
5. Fetch children from school or extra mural activities if possible but charge for this extra service.

Forecast

If you baby/pet sit three times a week at R100 per sitting you will make R1200 per month. However remember that you will be sitting for various clients and your clientele will increase on a weekly basis as word gets around that you are more than a baby sitter. Also research the hourly rate of baby/pet sitting and stick to your hourly rate; you will make more money that way.

46. Hemp By-Products

Hemp comes from the *Cannabis* family and is an extremely versatile plant. Products that are made from hemp include paper, rope, clothing, hemp oil, hemp milk etc…
Unfortunately due to the laws in South Africa this product is banned from agricultural production because of its association with cannabis. However hemp cannot be smoked and does not pose a threat to citizens as a drug. The production and sale of hemp can result in thousands of jobs as well as a boost to the South African export market. Hemp is imported into South Africa and it's by products are sold here however it is a largely untapped market.

Outlay

1. Hemp
2. Telephone
3. Computer
4. Advertising costs
5. Equipment and machinery

How, What, Where, When, Who

1. Hemp is sourced mostly from China, Canada and France. You can research and investigate cheaper suppliers.
2. Create opportunities to craft products from the hemp plant.
3. Use your knowledge and business expertise to teach people about the benefits of hemp.
4. Make designer clothing from hemp fabric and market its longevity (the more cotton is worn the more worn out it becomes whereas hemp becomes more enhanced and improved as it is worn).

5. Market the health as well as medicinal aspects of hemp products.

X-Factor: <u>What makes your business different?</u>

1. Start a drive to educate people about the uses of hemp. These products must become more visible. The more visible it becomes the more the demand will grow.
2. Invent new products from hemp, e.g. furniture and join the proudly South African family.
3. Join the growing number of campaigners and activists to influence the government to change its laws about the production of hemp in this country.
4. Keep up to date with scientific and agricultural investigations concerning the hemp plant and remember to keep the public informed.
5. Encourage publishers and printers to use hemp paper as it will save trees and protect our environment.

<u>Forecast</u>

As a result of this market being so untapped and under utilized you will have very few competitors. Your challenge will be to educate the population to become consumers of these very valuable products. Find out what the laws in your own country are regarding hemp production and start a campaign to make this product more usable and more visible.

47. Clairvoyance and Mediumship

Clairvoyance and mediumship takes years and years of training and meditation. Clairvoyance is the ability to see things that others cannot, mediumship is the ability to communicate with loved ones in the spirit world. If you are a gifted clairvoyant or medium why not use this gift to start your own business.

Outlay

1. Telephone
2. Meditation space
3. Consultation room

How, What, Where, When, Who

1. Many people need advice about current and future happenings and events in their lives. This is where a clairvoyant can be a valuable resource.
2. A clairvoyant can also give advice on business and personal relationships and events, especially where the client suspects something is amiss but does not have enough evidence.
3. A medium is consulted when a client wants to make contact with a loved one in the spirit world and this can bring about enormous closure and release of grief and guilt.
4. A medium can also assist a client to forge a better relationship with a loved one in spirit.
5. Advertise your services in holistic magazines and at holistic fares.
6. Ask a local radio station if you can have a slot on one of their shows in order to give free messages to their listeners.
7. Rent a room in a quiet space to do readings and sittings for clients. Alternatively use a quiet room in your house but do

not use that room for anything else and make sure that you clear it out by burning African Sage and incense regularly in order to remove any negative energy and to raise the frequency.

X-factor: <u>What makes your business?</u>

1. Not many people have this gift or talent.
2. You can teach people to enhance their psychic and intuitive abilities, which incidentally we all have albeit dormant.
3. Start a meditation circle.
4. Offer your services for kitchen teas, bachelor parties, office and corporate functions.
5. Assist the police in criminal investigations.

<u>Forecast</u>

If you work five days a week and see two clients per day charging a fee of R250 each, you will earn R2500 per week, which translates to R10 000 per month. This work can be highly rewarding especially as you receive positive feedback on your predictions.

48. Story Telling

Story telling is such an ancient tradition, which is found in many cultures across the globe. This tradition seems to be dying out especially with the advancement of media technology. You would need a love and natural ability for the spoken word and possibly a drama background.

Outlay

1. Various story books
2. Advertising costs

How, What, Where, When, Who

1. Create stories about families in ancient traditions.
2. Create stories about animals and their behaviour and how they relate to human experiences. Use analogies that children can relate to.
3. Create stories about humans, animals and plants and use them as analogies for the business world, teenagers and adults.
4. Tell your stories to corporates, schools, radio etc.
5. Ensure that you have very good voice control and that you can impersonate all types of voices, animal sounds and foreign accents.
6. Use your body to mimic human and animal behaviour.
7. Market your skills by advertising your concept to schools, radio, children's shows, corporate events, children's hospitals and wards, crèches, adult and children's parties etc.
8. Get yourself onto a TV talk show and register yourself with an event booking agent, so that people know where to contact you if they want to use your services.

X-Factor: <u>What makes your business different?</u>

1. This is a largely untapped market.
2. Your business can bring many smiles, laughs and life lessons to people.
3. Laughter is the best medicine and when sick children in hospital wards laugh they are sure to feel better.
4. You can take your business around the country and globe so travel becomes an interesting part of this business.
5. You could do voice over work for a puppet company, TV and film production.

<u>Forecast</u>

This can become such a gratifying business and will not even feel like you are working. You'll be having fun most of the time and bringing laughs and entertainment to others. Research what the going rate is for public appearances and based on that decide how many gigs per week you would like to perform.

49. Bargain Hunter

You would need to have a network of suppliers and know when and where products go on sale. You need to have an astute mind as well as transport to get to the bargains before they are sold out.

Outlay

1. A vehicle
2. A network of contacts
3. A computer
4. A cellular phone

How, What, Where, When, Who

1. You need to have the courage and ability to bargain with suppliers in order to get cheaper prices.
2. You also need to know the difference between a poor quality product and a good quality product.
3. Become familiar with brand names as well as generic names.
4. You could bargain hunt for clothing, accessories, home accessories, building materials, stationery, food, baby products and books etc.
5. You could purchase your bargain products and resell them. Alternatively you can advertise your services to clients and find them the items that they are looking for at cost price. You could then charge them a percentage or commission.
6. Start marketing your services with family and friends and remember to ask clients to refer you.
7. Start a social networking site where you track your bargains and advertise to your community. Remember to add photos' of your bargain purchases.

X-Factor: <u>What makes your business different?</u>

1. Once you know where to source products from you could leave out the middleman and go directly to the manufacturer, thus getting your client an even better deal.
2. Remember to attend auctions and visit junk shops where you can sometimes find incredible bargains.
3. The hunt begins when a client asks you to source a particular product and this can be such an adrenalin rush when you do manage to source the product, especially if it's found in an unusual place.
4. Become familiar with Internet sale sites such as Gumtree, eBay etc.
5. Source your products from home industries and especially home industries in third world countries.

<u>Forecast</u>

If you sell one item per day and ask for a percentage commission you could make a decent living. Sourcing products from manufacturers could add a new dimension to your business.

50. Calligrapher

Calligraphy is a skill that anyone can learn. Get yourself a good calligraphy set and practice until you feel comfortable to make your own products.

Outlay

1. A calligraphy set
2. Assorted pens
3. Metallic pens
4. Good quality card paper

How, What, Where, When, Who

1. You could design your own cards, wedding invitations and funeral leaflets etc.
2. If you are doing bulk sales such as funeral leaflets, only make one leaflet, scan it into your computer and make copies or take it to a print shop and have copies made.
3. The artwork on the front of the card does not need to be fancy. You could do geometric shapes, splashes of colour; stickmen, kiddie art etc. Remember that anything is art as long as it comes from a place of honest intention.
4. Market your product to family and friends, work colleagues, church groups, schools, hospitals, the Internet and social media etc.
5. Market your services to funeral parlours and event management companies.

X-Factor: What makes your business different?

1. Your cards are unusual because they have everyday "sayings" in them that people can relate to.

2. Your artwork is completely unassuming and unpretentious. You make it look so easy.
3. Your calligraphy is like poetry. You invent your own rhymes, poetry and put pen to paper.
4. You also do foreign language calligraphy for foreign language speakers.
5. Once a month you host a calligraphy class where you teach people to do calligraphy.
6. You make Christmas cards, birthday cards, get well cards, apology cards, proposal cards, wedding invitations, funeral leaflets, congratulatory cards, baby cards, certificates, scrolls which can also be framed etc.
7. You could also sell your product to retail stores and educational institutions.

Forecast

If you make two bulk sales of 100 each per month at R500 each and you sell 20 cards per month at R20 each, that amounts to R1400. If you host one workshop per month with 10 people in attendance at R50 each you will earn R500. This amounts to R1900 per month. Remember that you will make more money from foreign language cards, Internet sales, retail sales etc. This is a very creative business and the money will follow your passion.

Connecting with the author

Thank you for reading *50 Simple Business Ideas To Make Money*. I am availing my online services to you should you wish to make contact with me about your business idea. Remember that a business idea never remains stagnant; it grows and changes with the market trends and with the consumer's behaviour. I encourage you to use the business ideas in this book and to change it according to your circumstances, skills, niche market and available resources. I invite you to visit my website www.bernadettelundall.co.za and to communicate with me via email or on my blog. I would be very happy to help you grow and develop your business with my constructive guidance and intuition. I wish you all well with your endeavours and remember never to give up until you find the right business idea. Persevere with passion!!!

Resources

www.standardbank.co.za/bizconnect
www.tips-homebasedbusiness.info
www.motherearthnews.com
www.smallbusiness.chron.com
www.monkeydish.com
www.wikihow.com
www.theauctionwhisperer.com
www.artofmanliness.com
www.Fermentarium.com/industry
www.ecolechocolat.com
www.candletech.com
www.fabjob.com/matchmaker.asp
www.fromnaturalwithlove.com/reprint/inhomeskincarebusiness.asp
www.ecosystemgardening.com
www.hempworld.com
www.collective-evolution.com
www.storynet.org/resources/howtobecomeastoryteller.html

www.ingramcontent.com/pod-product-compliance
Lightning Source LLC
Chambersburg PA
CBHW060046210326
41520CB00009B/1283